SURVIVING YOUR YOUR ADOLESCENTS

THIRD EDITION

Thomas W. Phelan, Ph.D.

D1052696

ParentMagic, Inc.
Glen Ellyn, Illinois

Illustrations by Rex Bohn
Graphic Design by Mary Navolio
Distributed by Independent Publishers Group

Printed in the United States of America
10 9 8 7 6 5 4 3 2

For more information, contact:
ParentMagic, Inc.
800 Roosevelt Road, B309
Glen Ellyn, Illinois 60137

Publisher's Cataloging-in-Publication
(Provided by Quality Books, Inc.)

Phelan, Thomas W., 1943-
    Surviving your adolescents : how to manage--and let go of--your 13-18 year olds / Thomas W. Phelan. -- 3rd ed.
        p. cm.
        Includes index.
        ISBN 978-1-889140-60-5

    1. Parent and teenager. 2. Adolescent psychology.
3. Child rearing. 4. Teenagers.   I. Title.

HQ799.15.P44 2012   649'.125
                                       QBI12-600073

SURVIVING YOUR ADOLESCENTS

How to Manage and *Let Go Of* Your 13–18 Year Olds

THIRD EDITION

Other Materials by Thomas W. Phelan, Ph.D.

Surviving Your Adolescents
How to Manage—and *Let Go Of*—Your 13-18-Year Olds
DVD

1-2-3 Magic
Managing Difficult Behavior in Children 2-12
4th Edition
DVDs, Book and CD

1-2-3 Magic DVDs and book also available in Spanish

1-2-3 Magic for Teachers
Effective Classroom Discipline Pre-K through Grade 8
Book and DVD

1-2-3 Magic for Kids
Helping Your Children Understand the New Rules
Book
Also available in Spanish

All About Attention Deficit Disorder
Symptoms, Diagnosis and Treatment:
Children and Adults
Book and DVD

To order, visit **www.123Magic.com**
or call **1-800-442-4453**.

CONTENTS

The Snub

If you have a teenager, you've probably had an encounter like this at one time or other. After a long workday for you—and long school day for your sixteen-year-old son—it's dinnertime. You're trying to start a pleasant conversation.

Dead end—so far. But you're not about to give up that easily.

That's it. This same thing seems to go on every night.

When you ask your nine-year-old daughter about her day, on the other hand, you get the Complete Evening News. Extended and enthusiastic self-revelation is no problem for her.

Your sixteen-year-old son is different. He's quiet, even sullen-looking sometimes. "What am I doing wrong!?" you wonder. "All I'm trying to do is have a little talk. Is that too much to ask? What's wrong with this kid!?"

Parenting: Then and Now

Some of you have come to *Surviving Your Adolescents* by way of *1-2-3 Magic: Effective Discipline for Children 2-12*. From the time the kids were toddlers through their tween years (9-12), you used the relatively simple and straightforward strategies described in the "1-2-3" to both maintain reasonable control over the children's behavior and also to be able to enjoy their company.

Now that you have a teenager or two, however, you notice things are changing. Parenting during the *1-2-3 Magic* years (THEN), when the youngsters were 2-12, had a number of important differences from parenting during the *Surviving Your Adolescents* years (NOW), when the "kids" are 13-19 or so (or even way beyond). Let's look at these differences:

THEN   **NOW**

The Kids

THEN: *The kids are cute and engaging.*

NOW: *The children are strange-looking and often seem sullen or irritated.*

The little ones enjoy and seek out your company, and they seem to think that their parents know everything. The children are quite impressed by their parents' abilities and they like to emulate and imitate these strengths.

The teens, on the other hand, avoid parent contact and think it's absolutely uncool to be seen with Mom or Dad in public. Adolescents are frequently critical of their parents' behavior, feeling their parents are out of touch with reality.

Control

THEN: *Small children are helpless; you are the biggest influence in their lives.*

NOW: *The teens control most of their own behavior; peers, technology and media have more influence than you do.*

During the *1-2-3 Magic* years the kids are quite helpless, especially as infants, and you are the largest influence in their lives. If you don't like what they're doing, you can pick them up and put them somewhere else or use clever distraction or "redirection" tactics.

If you don't like what the adolescents are doing, you can't physically move them and you can't distract them. If you criticize the kids' activities or even make well-intended suggestions for improvement, you are met with argument or rolling eyes.

Parent Energy Level

THEN: *You are fresh, young and motivated; your parenting job is just beginning.*

NOW: *You are older, more tired and have other things to worry about; your parenting job is 70 percent or more over.*

Sure, younger kids can be exhausting (frequently!), but your physical and mental condition usually allows you to be up to the challenge. Parenting is new and its challenges are often—though not always—rewarding. You enjoy talking to friends about your children as well as theirs.

SYA years find you with a distinct change in energy level. Though you keep going at a good pace, you don't have the extra energy you used to have. You also have a number of other things to worry about, such as your own physical and mental health, the health of your parents, your job, marital issues and perhaps financial concerns.

Your Job Description

THEN: *Your parenting job is straightforward.*
NOW: *What is your job at this point, anyway?*

Your task used to be to control obnoxious behavior, encourage good behavior, and strengthen your relationship with the kids.

In just a few years, however, your teenagers will be leaving home. You look forward to that huge event and fear it at the same time. What are you supposed to do with them in the meantime?

Where To Start

Adolescents present their parents with a number of puzzling and difficult situations—just like The Snub described above. That's the bad news. The good news is this: If you can *understand and accept* the causes of The Snub itself, you're halfway home when it comes to living with and "managing" a teenager.

Believe it or not.

"I don't know what to do with this kid anymore," many moms and dads grumble regarding their teens. That's what this book is about: Exactly what should you "do" with your adolescents. And—equally important—what should you not do with them!

Before you try to do anything it is essential that you understand several things, so the next part of this book is called Straight Thinking. First, it is critical that you appreciate (and remember!) what adolescence is like, what is pretty much normal teen behavior, and why and how teens take risks (Chapters 1-3). Then you need to recognize how your teenage son or daughter's behavior *makes you think and feel* (Chapter 4). Trying to accomplish anything without this knowledge is like trying to drive at night without your headlights.

Then comes the Bottom Line: your New Job Description as the parent of an adolescent. In Chapter 5 I'll offer you a basic template for the profession. The job proposal has five pieces. Each of the next five parts of *Surviving Your Adolescents* (Parts II-VI) will deal with one of these pieces.

Surviving Your Adolescents is not about theory; it's about changing things at your house. In accomplishing this change it will help you— like, a whole lot!—if you can recall *your* life as a teenager. What serious issues did you think about, how did you behave, how did you feel about your parents, and what kinds of things did you do that your parents knew nothing about?

In appreciating your teens, it will also be of great assistance if you know something about the lyrics to the music they like. Music lyrics are easily found on the internet.

What's this kid thinking about? Let's find out!

PART I

Straight Thinking

CHAPTER 1
Appreciating Adolescence

CHAPTER 2
What's Normal?

CHAPTER 3
Risky Business

CHAPTER 4
Diagnosing Your Own Reactions

CHAPTER 5
Your New Job Description

CHAPTER 1

Appreciating Adolescence

Somewhere between perhaps fourth grade and high school, it gradually dawns on your kids that life is presenting them with a big job to do. Or rather, big jobs to do. Your kids don't necessarily see these things as jobs; they just see them as part of life. These Herculean tasks are the essence of growing up and they're the same ones that you had to deal with when you were young.

Often listed under the banner of "establishing one's identity" or "proving oneself," these daunting assignments include the following:

1. Making sense out of life: the world, other people and yourself
2. Finding and keeping friends
3. Finding and keeping a sex/soulmate
4. Establishing a job/career
5. Physically leaving home and establishing economic independence
6. Discovering how to enjoy life on a daily basis

As time goes on, your children come to realize that these tasks have to be done largely alone. No one, no matter how well-meaning, (not even parents), can do these things for anyone else. But the teens also realize that all their friends are in the same boat. This fact provides reassurance as well as—off and on—a disturbing sense of competition.

Teenagers have mixed feelings about life's assignments for two reasons. First, they're not sure they can live up to all these challenges and wind up being reasonably happy. TV, movies, religion, parents and politics all present drastically different views of the world and of human beings. In addition, you can't control the behavior of would-be friends and it's hard to even understand—much less control—the behavior of the opposite sex! The idea of leaving home may become more and more attractive as the kids get older, but adolescents often have little idea as to how that job can or will be accomplished.

Second, teenagers aren't sure they *want* to accept all these tasks, especially items 4 and 5. Pink Floyd once sang, "Welcome my son, welcome to the machine. Where have you been?" Isn't the machine the lair of "The Man" and "The Establishment"? Isn't The Man the head of The Establishment, which was put into place to exploit people and bring them down? And isn't The Man probably a male Caucasian who has acquired quite a bit of wealth through questionable activities and who is not about to share it? So who in their right mind would want to join all the phonies in The Establishment in the first place?

But, then again, if you don't join, where does that leave you? Unfortunately, kids in our society have a lot of time—from the ages of eleven to about twenty-two or so—to mull over this dilemma.

Sex and Soulmate

While the friend and career issues are very important, the sex/soulmate-finding problem is obsessive during the adolescent years. The problem is infinitely compounded, it seems, by new feelings regarding sex and romance (for the boys) and romance and sex (for the girls). Strangely, many parents of teens are not only unsympathetic but often critical of their sons' or daughters' goofy romantic behavior.

Adolescents know there are two parts to the sex/soulmate problem. The first is finding your companion. As Madonna (and a few million others) have pointed out, falling in love is quite a high:

> *It's all brand new,*
> *I'm crazy for you*
> *And you know it's true*
> *I'm crazy, crazy for you*

Unfortunately, falling in love and finding someone to love is only the first (and probably the easiest) part of the game. The second and harder part of the job is keeping the person you found. The history of music if chock full of painful stories about relationships gone wrong. Here's Elvis:

> *Well, since my baby left me,*
> *I found a new place to dwell.*
> *It's down at the end of lonely street*
> *At Heartbreak Hotel.*

"Job and career (and this nuisance called school) can wait for a while. I have more important things to worry about: relationships or the lack thereof." If you could magically examine the stream of consciousness of teen boys and girls, you would find that massive amounts of thought and emotion are tied up with the romance and with sex itself. Reciprocated love can provide one of life's greatest thrills; unreciprocated love can generate some of life's lowest lows. Soulmate-finding is a world of intense excitement and intense anxiety.

The mind of the adolescent, in many ways then, is occupied more with imaginations than with actual experience. The dreams about the future are both exciting and frightening and they are always instantly available. But since the fantasies are not realities yet, these dreams can produce a painful sense of inadequacy and frustration. The career that might come later does not exist now and might not even be chosen. The unidentified love of one's life may be unknowingly wandering around out there  somewhere. Or she might not exist and a life of loneliness might be ahead. What can be done now about all these concerns? You wait and then wait some more. In the meantime, how about a little *Grand Theft Auto?*

Prolooooonged Adolescence Means Insult

Adding insult to injury for most adolescents is the fact that their "teen-age" years last so long. Adolescence for many "youngsters" is not simply the ages thirteen to eighteen; it really encompasses the years from age eleven (for many girls the onset of puberty) to age twenty-two (the completion of college) or even longer. During these years a young man or woman may still be dependent upon older adults for food, shelter, clothing and warmth, as well as for some (often unwanted) direction and supervision. This situation may persist even though the young person may be biologically and mentally capable of managing a lot more herself.

Of all the animals on earth, the human spends the largest portion of its total life span (approximately one quarter to one third) with its parents before achieving final independence. Bugs, fish, birds and even monkeys live with their parents for only a relative fraction of the time human offspring do.

And of all the countries on earth, the more modern, industrialized nations—such as the United States—keep their kids under foot for the longest period of time. This stretched-out and difficult period of dependence is due to the extended time required to educate children for the more complicated, skilled jobs and careers that are characteristic of industrial countries. There is first a high school diploma, then perhaps an associate's or bachelor's degree. Then how about an MBA, Ph.D., M.D., M.S., R.N. or J.D.?

DO YOU REMEMBER?

- Your favorite song at 13?
- Your feelings eating dinner with family and parents?
- Your thoughts about the opposite sex?
- Job/career ideas?

It hasn't always been like this. Anthropologists long ago pointed out that in simpler societies the transition from childhood to adulthood was usually much shorter and, in a few cultures, "adolescence" hardly existed at all. One day you're a kid, and then wham! after a brief ceremony or "rite of passage," you're an adult—ready or not—with all the privileges and responsibilities of other adults in your community. Here's your boat, knife and fishing net—go get 'em!

The Sioux Indians, for example, had carefully designed rites of passage for males who might become warriors. Some of these rites involved piercing your own chest with devices that were attached to cords hung from a tall pole. The initiate then dangled from the cords and danced in the air until the cords ripped out of their torn flesh. Those surviving the ceremony were consequently recognized as adult warriors, their courage, bravery and new role appreciated and admired by themselves and the other members of their tribe. The duration of adolescence here? Just a few days.

Contrast this state of affairs with that of Holden Caulfield in *The Catcher in the Rye*. After perhaps four or five years of adolescence, Holden has no meaningful view of life, no real friends, no sex/soulmate, no realistic thoughts about job or career, certainly no economic independence or even a place to live, and no real expertise when it comes to enjoying himself. And he's only about halfway through his teenage years. No wonder he feels anxious and depressed.

The Sioux warrior did not have to endure a seemingly never-ending, directionless existence. That's probably one reason why enlisting in the military service is appealing to some young men and women today. Instant self-respect and the admiration of pretty much everyone around you. Holden had only his hunting cap.

Insult Means Irritation and Alienation

Generally speaking, though, rapid rites of passage, straightforward role definitions and positive public recognition during one's adolescence are hard to come by. In the United States, as well as other modern nations, privilege and responsibility are dished out piecemeal to the new adult/child between the approximate ages of thirteen and twenty-one. Now you can manage your own money and choose your own clothes. Now you can drive. Now you can date, go to work or leave school. Now you can legally vote or drink or stay out past midnight. What about sex? Many adults feel young people should delay sexual gratification for a long, long time.

Our society has not yet found a way to deal with the fact that prolonged dependence is insulting to young people. Many teens feel they're ready for adult responsibilities and privileges long before parents and society are willing to let the adolescents tackle them. For some kids these youthful perceptions may be correct, while for others these views may be off base. Doesn't make any difference: The inevitable result of prolonged adolescence in our culture is that teens will regularly feel irritation toward older folks and a sense of alienation from the society they are a part of.

The result of this irritation and alienation includes a desire to rebel, to do things differently, to pull back from and to criticize the ways of parents and other adults. After all, aren't most adults and most parents part of the conforming, impersonal, unfulfilling, unemotional and man-eating machine? In some kids, especially where serious family conflict exists, the impatience and frustration of adolescence can contribute to underachievement, vandalism, drug misuse and other kinds of dangerous risk-taking behavior. Whatever form it takes, this oppositional stance is one way for youngsters to both maintain their self-respect—while still in a semi-dependent state—and distance themselves from their unwanted caretakers.

It's also part of what's behind The Snub.

CHAPTER 2

What's Normal?

You take a deep breath and you walk through the doors,
It's the morning of your very first day.

– Taylor Swift, *Fifteen*

Given the protracted unrest we described in the last chapter, what can we expect teens to be like? One of the toughest parts of being the parent of a teenager is trying to figure out which aspects of your kids' behavior are trouble and which are normal. Some days it seems that most of what teens do is strange, aggravating and worlds apart from the way they used to act. Whatever happened to that easygoing nine-year-old you I used to enjoy so much?

In this chapter we'll describe the characteristics you can reasonably expect to see in your normal, average teenager (if there is such a creature!). Anticipating these features can help you in several ways. First of all, this awareness tells you that these new traits are common and not necessarily dangerous. Second, knowing what's normal can liberate you from taking these qualities personally—as if they were your fault, or as if they represented some kind of personal rejection. Finally, memorizing this list will get you to work on one of the primary jobs of the parent of an adolescent: toleration of nonessential differences.

Self-Consciousness

Younger adolescents become extremely focused on their own thoughts, feelings and activities. In fact, some writers have pointed out that it's almost as if the child feels she is constantly on stage in front of some imaginary audience. She may feel that her own experiences are so intense and unique that no one else—least of all her parents—could possibly understand what she is going through. In feeling misunderstood, teens forget that their parents were adolescents once, too.

Can you recall speech class in high school? It would be very unusual if you couldn't! Did you ever consider ditching school on the day of the presentation? How many weeks in advance did you worry about the possibility of making a complete fool of yourself in front of your peers?

In a sense, though, the kids have a point, because many parents react impulsively to their adolescent offspring and don't take the time to recall what it was like when they were that age. Parents may complain that "she's too wrapped up in her own little world" without remembering what that "little world" was like for themselves a while back.

While extreme self-consciousness may be egocentric, this orientation toward life is also a burden. If everything revolves around me and the whole world is watching, that feeling is very, very uncomfortable. The adolescent may feel that her successes are marvelous and amazing—testimonials to her incredible ability and potential. "Way cool!" On the other hand, failure or being criticized, especially in front of others, can be excruciating. "That's just great. Now everyone will think I'm a total dork!" In high school an adolescent's worst fear is embarrassment or humiliation in front of her peers.

Rapid Change

Adolescence is a time of multiple, massive changes. Some of these changes take years, while others seem to occur almost overnight. Some changes are exciting, while others may be bewildering or even upsetting for teens and parents alike.

> *He's not concerned with yesterday*
> *He knows constant change is here today.*
>
> – Rush, *New World Man*

Physically the body of an adolescent will change more than it will at any other time of life except infancy. From the beginning to the end of puberty, adolescents on the average add ten inches in height and 40 pounds in weight. The growth spurt for girls begins around age 11, on the average, and is completed by age 16. Girls' hips broaden relative to their shoulders and waist, and they tend to add more fat on their arms, legs and torso. The growth spurt for boys starts around age 13 and continues until about age 17-1/2. Boys' shoulders broaden relative to their waists, and they develop larger skeletal muscles while decreasing arm and leg fat.

During puberty, sex hormones start to do their thing. Perspiration, oiliness of the skin and hair, and body odor all increase. Sex hormones also see to it that primary and secondary sexual characteristics develop. Teens do not always greet these physical events with enthusiasm. Girls react to the arrival of their first period with surprise and mixed emotions that depend, in part, upon how much support they receive from family members and how much prior information they have. Boys usually have more advance information before they experience their first ejaculation, but in general they receive less support for the physical changes of puberty than do girls.

While the physical changes mentioned above take a few years, it may seem to parents that some of the nonphysical changes occur overnight. One day, without warning, the child's bedroom door shuts and stays shut. During one summer month the youngster seems to have become glued to a new set of friends, and suddenly he couldn't care less about family affairs.

Sometimes adolescent change goes back and forth. One day the girl is friendly, warm and fun. The next day she is moody and distant for no identifiable reason. You have a hard time making sense out of her frequent bouts of ambivalence. Anthony Wolf's recent book about teenagers is entitled *Get Out of My Life, but First Could You Drive Me & Cheryl to the Mall?* Whatever the case, change is a large part of the teen years, and Mom and Dad's understanding and tolerance of the non-dangerous alterations in their offsprings' appearance, thinking and behavior is an important part of the tricky new art of parenting.

Shock Value and Weirdness

Teens love weirdness and shock value: strange sounds, colors, clothes, posters. Being different—from adults but not necessarily from each other—becomes an important goal in their daily activities. Forging an identity certainly does not mean slavish imitation of your own mother or father! It also helps to keep your parents confused and off-balance:

> *His palms are sweaty, knees weak, arms are heavy*
> *There's vomit on his sweater already, mom's spaghetti*
> *He's nervous, but on the surface he looks calm and*
> *   ready to drop bombs...*
>
> — Eminem, *Lose Yourself*

What was that again!? While in a grocery check-out line one day, I was struck by the appearance of the young girl who was ringing up the orders. Though she had a very pleasant personality, her hair was amazingly unconventional. Half of her head was sporting a blue crew cut, while the other half had spiked, orange hair. While gazing at this remarkable display, I found myself trying to decide if she had been pretty before she had done this to herself.

Nowhere, perhaps, does shock value play a greater role than in the realm of music. It may be true that all generations think the music of the next generation is terrible. But as the decades go by, what was shocking at one time becomes commonplace in later years, and artists have to go to greater and greater extremes to accomplish the twin goals of pleasing teens and traumatizing parents. Music groups seem to be continually searching for the extreme when it comes to both loudness and lyrics. And while moms and dads may find these musical productions obnoxious, their teenage sons and daughters love them.

Emotional and Physical Distance

Parents will find their teens are becoming more and more distant from them, both physically and emotionally. The child doesn't want to eat dinner with the family as often as before. She is less interested in going out with you as well, whether it's for dinner, to a movie or for family get-togethers.

Privacy becomes more important to the adolescent. Her door is now shut more of the time, and you're left wondering what's going on in there now that wasn't happening before. It's certainly not all homework! The kid seems to have to be constantly "wired" to her friends. The meanderings of younger brothers or sisters into your teenage daughter's bedroom may be met with bursts of temper and demands to be left alone.

Communication also isn't the same. Where you used to sit around and shoot the breeze after dinner, now the youngster is gone, having said hardly anything. She doesn't tell you as much as she did before about things that bother or excite her, though she appears to be able to communicate very energetically by cell phone, Facebook or text for hours with friends. Innocent questions from you are often met with an attitude of irritation or suspicion, as if you were unjustly prying into her affairs.

Your daughter is showing more and more independence. For one thing, she is simply not home as much as before. It's nice she has a job, but between that and her friends, you hardly ever see her. Your suggestion that the two of you go out shopping for clothes is met with an icy stare. She'd rather do that on her own.

Just because teens cannot leave home yet physically does not mean they can't leave home mentally.

A Passion for Peers

Your son's social focus has shifted dramatically—away from home and toward friends. During his spare time he wants to go out with his buddies. He seems to have little time for family, or for you, or for doing what he's supposed to around the house. Essential tasks like cutting the grass don't get done, but there seems to be plenty of time for apparently frivolous encounters with friends. Half of these kids you haven't even met, and some of those you have met you're not at all sure you like.

When a romantic relationship develops, it is positively obsessive. Long and extremely private conversations on the phone are followed by starry-eyed wonder or unexplained moodiness. The question "Is there something wrong?" inspires a snarl and a not-too-gentle hint that you should mind your own business. When—God forbid—a romantic relationship ends after months of breakups and tearful reunions, you find yourself unable to sleep at night, worrying about depression and suicidal potential.

Inexperience and Idealism

Teens have not had a lot of experience in testing dreams against reality. They have not been around the block a few times like you have. Two of the blocks in particular your kids have not experienced (and you  have) include first, long-term sex/soulmate relationships with their ups and downs and, second, long-term job or career experience.

The inexperience of adolescence does not at all mean that teens have no opinions. On the contrary, they can be quite opinionated and some of their notions may seem crazy. Someone once said, "If you want to get something done, give it to a teenager while they still know everything." Teens have quite a few ideas about how the world—as well as their family, school and country—should be run. They may come across as budding trial attorneys when they evaluate the activities of their elders.

> *Another member of the crowd goes down to drown at the liquor store*
> *Choose your escape in the heartland*
> *Of product and demand when you feel like a wasp in the swarm*
> *You gotta get away any way that you can*
>
> — Operation Ivy, *Artificial Life*

That's why one of the top complaints from parents about their teenage sons and daughters is that the kids argue too much. Arguing is a two-way street, however, and it's a mistake to throw all your kids' ideas in the trash. If you calm down and listen to your teens and to their music sometimes, you'll find many valid ideas and some good suggestions, both for you and for the world today.

Risk-Taking

Adolescents are experimenters. We worry about their driving, drug use, smoking, drinking, sexual activity and use of technology. Some teens can be dangerously creative. One study of adolescent mortality, for example, reported a number of teenage deaths due to skateboarding under the influence of alcohol.

Much adolescent risk-taking, of course, is due to a natural and healthy curiosity about life. There are so many fascinating new experiences to be discovered! Teenage experimentation also results from the urge to do things differently from one's parents. "Mom and Dad are such a drag; don't they ever have any fun? I'm going to do things my way and enjoy life."

> *He's got to make his own mistakes*
> *And learn to mend the mess he makes*
> *He's old enough to know what's right*
> *But young enough not to choose it...*
>
> — Rush, *New World Man*

Some risk-taking also results from the egocentric adolescent view that one has unique awareness and special abilities that will not allow injury. Even though teens are at a point where they can intellectually appreciate the possible consequences of certain behavior, they don't always "put two and two together" when it comes down to their own actions. Sadly, every year thousands of teen pregnancies and auto fatalities are caused, in part, by this unfounded sense of invulnerability.

Worries about teen risk-taking occupy a significant portion of parents' consciousness. And teens' increasing reluctance to communicate makes parents even more suspicious that bad things might be happening. So in the next chapter let's see if we can take a fairly calm look at adolescent risk-taking.

CHAPTER 3

Risky Business

Danger, danger, give me danger, danger
Give me measures of pleasure and pain.
— Kiss, *Danger*

ortunately, the vast majority of teens are not crazed, thrill-chasing
dangerphiles. Their video games may be as close as they come to
significant peril. Nevertheless, prompted by curiosity, peer influences,
sensation-seeking and a host of other factors, adolescents will experiment with risky behavior that ranges from minor to serious and from
the trivial to the sublime. Teens may be curious to see what happens if
they cut a class, cut themselves, stay up all night, try out some weird
clothes, don a new hair style or even a different kind of personality.

From their parents' perspective, the most consistently worrisome
risk-taking teens engage in involves the "Big Four": driving, drug and
alcohol use, sex and involvement with technology. The possibility for
adolescent injury or death presented by these four threats, naturally,
produces strong anxiety in mothers and fathers of teenagers. This
parental anxiety, in its turn, can cause its own problems, including not
only sleepless nights for parents but also extremely negative effects

23

on the parent/teen relationship itself. And as we'll see, a worsening of this adult/adolescent relationship increases the chances of the kid's getting hurt.

Driving

Each year motor vehicle accidents by themselves account for almost forty percent of adolescent deaths. We sometimes forget this gruesome statistic, but insurance companies do not. They charge their highest rates for the riskiest group of drivers, adolescent males, and their rates go even higher if the boy in question is not a particularly good student. Casualties due to automobile accidents involve more than just teenage drivers. They also include the passengers of adolescent-driven cars and motorcycles, as well as the pedestrians and the bicyclists—old as well as young—whom these kids kill or cripple.

Teens love the excitement, freedom and independence involved in taking the car out by themselves without Mom or Dad. Who wouldn't!? Most of us can recall our first times alone behind the wheel.

It was just an old hand-me-down Ford
With three-speed on the column and a dent in the door
Sit up in the seat and stretch my feet out to the pedals
Smiling like a hero that just received his medal.

– Alan Jackson, *Drive*

In a society where adolescence is so obnoxiously long, driving provides a chance to enjoy some true adult fun and responsibility. Unfortunately, at the time they acquire this privilege, sixteen-year olds have precious little driving experience. Yet lack of driving experience may not be so much of a factor in teen traffic fatalities as risky driving habits. Teens are famous for not using seatbelts, for speeding and for tailgating.

Adolescents are also known for drinking and driving. When a motor vehicle accident involves a fatality and a teenage driver, that teenage driver was drunk about fifty percent of the time. Use of alcohol as well as other drugs also plays an all-too-frequent role when teens die in accidents involving recreational vehicles.

Moms and dads also worry about their kids combining something else with driving: technology. Research has shown that using a cell phone while driving (handheld or hands-free) delays reaction times as much as having a blood alcohol level of .08—the legal limit. But when it comes to distracted driving, texting is worse than cell phone use. Texting takes your eyes off the road for an average of five seconds, and texting drivers are twenty-three times more likely to get into accidents than nontexting drivers. And the age group with the greatest proportion of distracted drivers is the under-twenty gang.

Drugs and Alcohol

Alcohol is fascinating stuff. What is this liquid that adults love, that they use so regularly and that can change their behavior so dramatically? What does it feel like to be high or drunk? Do you have more fun or do you just get sick? Can alcohol give you more self-confidence?

Curiosity combined with the encouragement of peers and factors such as low socioeconomic status, family conflict, poor school performance, parental drug use, lack of close friends and inconsistent monitoring has resulted in extremely high adolescent use of alcohol and other drugs in the United States—higher than in any other industrialized country. According to Laura Berk, author of *Child Development* (8th Edition), by the time they have, finished 10th grade, sixty-three per cent of kids report having tried alcohol, and twenty-eight per cent report heavy drinking in the last two weeks. By the time they are seniors in high school, about four percent of students are daily drinkers.

DO YOU REMEMBER?

When you were in high school, was there any peer pressure to drink, try marijuana or experiment with other drugs? If so, what were your thoughts about that? If you did not experiment, what kept you from doing that?

Smoking and the effects of nicotine are also of interest to adolescents seeking new experiences. Smoking is an "adult-like" thing to do, and it can even help wake you up and sometimes improve your concentration. By the end of 10th grade, forty percent of teens have tried smoking, and by the time they are seniors, 17 percent are regular cigarette smokers.

Adolescent use of illegal drugs is also extremely high in the U.S. as compared to other countries. By the time they leave high school, about forty percent have experimented with illegal substances, mostly marijuana. Twenty percent have tried highly addictive substances, including amphetamines, cocaine, PCP, inhalants, heroin and OxyContin (a prescription painkiller). And your kids hear stuff like this:

> If you got bad news, you wanna kick them blues; cocaine.
> When your day is done and you wanna run; cocaine.
> She don't lie, she don't lie, she don't lie; cocaine.

> – Eric Clapton, Cocaine

Though these figures represent an overall decline in illegal substance use over the last few years, use of sedatives, inhalants and OxyContin may have increased. For regular users, some drugs can provide kicks as well as anti-depressant effects, and a small but worrisome percentage of adolescents continue to "graduate" from experimentation to drug abuse, where drugs are regularly used to deal with daily life and painful emotions.

Sex and Romance

While growing up in the United States, a typical youngster will see on prime-time TV an average of three episodes per hour that involve spontaneous, romantic and unprotected sex—with no bad consequences! Advertisers exploit sex constantly on television, in magazines and on the internet. We may be fascinated with sex, but at the same time—believe it or not—the United States is much more conservative about sex than many other countries. Parents in this country rarely talk about the topic to, or in front of, their children, and they rarely give the kids much information about sex.

When moms and dads do broach the subject, it's often The Big Talk and then nothing. Big Talks also tend to focus on the physical and mechanical without discussing the interaction of sexual feelings with relationships and romance. Consequently, children turn to sources such as the web, movies, magazines and friends, where the quality of the information they receive is unpredictable.

Parental avoidance of sex discussions finds its polar opposite in the obsession with sex found in music and song. In the old days, songs were dominated by romance with hints of the physical possibilities:

You turn to me with a kiss in your eyes
And my heart feels a thrill beyond compare
Then your lips cling to mine, it's wonderful, wonderful
Oh, so wonderful my love.

— Johnny Mathis, *Wonderful, Wonderful*

As time went on, many song lyrics, perhaps inevitably, became way more sexually explicit than most parents liked. Often the focus switched to a focus on sex with—if you were lucky—a hint of romance.

No place for hidin', Baby
No place to run
You pull the trigger of my love gun...

— Kiss, *Love Gun*

What are the consequences of experiencing your sexual awakening in a sexually overstimulated society that refuses to discuss sex openly? Adolescents get hurt in two ways: unwanted pregnancy and sexually transmitted diseases. Among industrialized nations, the United States has a very high adolescent pregnancy rate, though it has decreased significantly in the last ten years. Each year over 800,000 teens become pregnant—the vast majority of them unmarried.

Papa don't preach, I'm in trouble deep
Papa don't preach, I've been losing sleep
But I made up my mind, I'm keeping my baby, oh
I'm gonna keep my baby...

— Madonna, *Papa Don't Preach*

In the U.S., forty percent of these girls decide on abortion as the solution, and another 13 percent of the pregnancies result in miscarriage. Surprisingly, very few teens choose to give up their babies for adoption. The result is that every year over hundreds of thousands of unmarried teenage girls become parents under the most difficult of circumstances and their babies enter the world at serious risk.

The other sex-related problem that causes consistent injury to teens is sexually transmitted disease. Adolescents in this country have the highest rate of STD of any age group. This statistic does not mean that all teens here are sexually promiscuous, though some certainly are. By the time they are eighteen years old, according to one study, about half of boys and girls in the U.S. will have been sexually active, but usually this behavior occurs in a monogamous relationship.

Kids get into trouble with sexually transmitted diseases for other reasons. For one thing, convenient, non-embarrassing and low-cost access to birth control devices is rare. Providing condoms or birth control pills to teens is also a very controversial issue. Some kids wrongly believe that oral contraceptives or oral sex can prevent STDs. And even when protection is available, teens don't always use it.

Often overlooked among the sexual issues that can impact adolescents is homosexuality. With their sexual awakening, a surprising proportion of teens will discover that they are attracted to the same sex. Some writers feel that children with a homosexual preference may represent up to four per cent of our adolescent population. The inclination toward the same sex in these teenagers is much stronger than in those adolescents who are simply experimenting with homosexuality, which is fairly common.

Homosexuality probably has a significant genetic basis and it is no longer considered a form of mental illness. Nevertheless, the strain a homosexual orientation puts on a young man or woman is tremendous, and the issue can present a painful dilemma for their parents.

Teens and Tech

Teens' daily consumption of mass communication by means of various tech devices gets larger and larger every year (ass does their parents'). Recent estimates tell us that over 7.5 hours per day are spent by 8–18 year olds with TV, cell phones, music, computer, video games, print and movies. Some people claim the real figure should be 10.5 hours, because about three of the daily tech hours are spent "multitasking," which means doing two or more things (TV, texting, surfing) at the same time.

The tech revolution is truly remarkable and it has brought a number of positive developments for society and your children. Unfortunately, technology also presents a number of troubling problems. Like driving, drugs and alcohol and sex, it too can be risky business. Violence is portrayed online, on TV, in the movies, and especially in video games. A typical news broadcast consists of 30 percent ads and 53 percent crime, disaster and war. By eighth grade, kids will have seen about 8,000 murders on TV; they will have committed quite a few murders themselves while gaming. Two-thirds of American homes own a video game console. Popular games include Dead Rising, where you fight waves of zombies, and Grand Theft Auto, where you fight to move up in the underworld.

Perhaps even more troubling is the pornography that is available through new technology. The average age of a child's first exposure to pornography is 11. According to Family Safe Media, the largest group of viewers of Internet porn is children between ages 12 and 17. Another danger is sexual predators. One in seven children who use the Internet regularly report receiving sexually suggestive remarks from someone they don't know, either online or through text messaging.

Sometimes online relationships are hurtful to teens through what is called cyberbullying: using technology to harass and victimize others. Some adolescents love to make fun of other kids. Since online abuse is not face-to-face, it is easier for youngsters to participate.

All the new technological innovations can also have a negative impact on parent/teen relations. Arguments can break out about time spent on video games, about cell phone usage and cost, or about the relevance of movie or game ratings. Making matters worse is the fact that in these battles, confident teens often know more about tech subjects than their nervous parents. In addition, kids often appreciate something that their parents don't: Today's tech devices change rapidly and their functions overlap considerably. Technology that once was just on the computer is now on the cell phone. What was once on a video game console is now on a handheld device, the computer and the cell phone.

Two other tech negatives are worth mentioning: lack of physical exercise and wasted time. Seven to ten hours per day per kid is a lot. It would be very, very beneficial for their future welfare if kids got into a habit of physical exercise at least one hour per day. Exercise helps you and your body deal with lots of stressors, so it is great for—and in many folks, essential for—your mental health.

What about wasted time? In addition, our teens are still preparing for their futures and their careers. In Malcolm Gladwell's bestselling book,

> **CAUTION**
>
> Be careful when discussing technology issues with your adolescents—they often know a lot more than you do! Think through and then state your opinions, but above all ask thoughtful questions and be a good listener.

The Outliers, the author describes his "10,000-Hour Rule." He says the key to success in any field is a matter of practicing a specific skill for a total of 10,000 hours. You want to be an excellent piano player? Practice for 10,000 hours. A great basketball player? Practice 10,000 hours.

If your kids do video games, TV and Internet for eight hours per day for fifteen years of their growing-up time in your home, they will have logged over 40,000 "techplay" hours.

Did they need that much recreation? According to *The Outliers*, your children could have become experts in four different areas over that same period. Imagine the possible effects on their future job, career and overall success. A risk here is a big opportunity cost—lost skills.

CHAPTER 4

Diagnosing Your Own Reactions

If your teen is acting like a pretty normal teenager, she is putting you in a funny and awkward position. And if you are a pretty normal parent, the adolescent's behavior will cause predictable thoughts, feelings and actions in you. That's where you have to start if you're going to come up with a new job description for yourself. You have to diagnose and understand your own reactions to the strange, new creature that is inhabiting your house.

A normal teenager will make you feel anxious about hazards involving driving, drugs and alcohol, sex and techy things like the internet. At the same time, when you look for information or reassurance, that same normal teen will not want to talk to you. Consequently, you wind up feeling both rejected as well as worried.

Did you know that your thoughts cause your feelings? Sure, what happens to you is important. But it's more how you interpret or think about what happens to you that determines how you feel. And how you feel, in turn, will have a big effect on what you do and how you behave. Let's apply this model to the dilemma faced by the typical, well-meaning, and mostly normal parent of an adolescent.

The Snub

In the Introduction we witnessed a sixteen-year old who did not want to answer the simple question, "How was your day?" (Don't say he answered it, because "fine" is not an answer.) Not answering simple, polite questions is one version of The Snub. But The Snub can also take other forms, such as keeping the bedroom door shut, not wanting to be seen with you in public, and having an enthusiastic tone of voice with friends but a matter-of-fact and somber one with you.

When you're being snubbed, you're likely to think these thoughts:

Thoughts cause feelings. These thoughts (generated by The Snub) will make you feel irritated or angry. Now hold that idea for a second while we continue.

Risk

Now let's look at the potential for teen experimentation and risk taking. Not only are you feeling left out, you are aware that your control over this youngster is slipping, and, in reality, it is. So now we have you thinking thoughts like these:

Thoughts cause feelings. The thoughts (generated by risk-taking potential) will make you feel anxious.

Now, there's a funny law of human nature that goes like this: If someone scares you or makes you nervous, you will get mad at them. Ever seen a mother whose two-year old just ran out into the street, or a Dad whose daughter comes home from school two hours late? Both of these parents are mad—in fact, they may be furious—but *before the anger came the fear.*

Rejection + Risk = Irritation + Anger

The bottom line is this: Both The Snub and teen risk-taking potential have the same effect on parents—*they make parents irritated and angry with their adolescents.* Some days are better and some are worse, but in general this irritation and anger will lead to certain predictable behavior on the part of moms and dads. Since the teen is already pulling away from Mom and Dad, the parents' behavior will further increase the hostility and distance. Increase the parent/child hostility and distance and you have a greater likelihood that the adolescents will get hurt.

What do irritated parents do? The list includes many of possibilities. Irritated parents:

1. Resnub. You won't talk to me, so why the hell should I talk to you!? Don't go out with me—I won't bother with you either.
2. Make irritable comments and engage in the Four Cardinal Sins (Chapter 11).
3. Become bad and biased listeners.
4. Grow to be extremely uncreative and rigid in approaching their teens; they repeatedly ask the same silly questions, such as "How was your day?"
5. Try to exercise control that does not exist.

Tragedy

Parental reactions such as these will continue to aggravate the hostility and distance barrier. This quiet standoff between parent and teen is a very unpleasant way to live—like the dinosaur-in-the-living-room kind of thing. More important than that, though, the parent/teen barrier is dangerous—*both for the teenager and for the community in which he lives.*

Quite a few years ago a young couple came to see me. Let's call them the Smiths. As they walked into the office, their manner was serious, subdued and sad. I asked what brought them and they told me this story.

A couple of months earlier they had gotten up on a Saturday summer morning and had gone out into the front yard to play with their two kids, a one-year-old boy and three-year-old girl. The couple lived in a fairly new subdivision in the suburbs. Unbeknownst to them, about the same time, in a house a few blocks away, a sixteen-year-old boy was concluding a ferocious argument with his parents. The argument had to do with his grades and the fact that he didn't like his parents trying to supervise his homework.

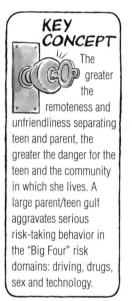

KEY CONCEPT The greater the remoteness and unfriendliness separating teen and parent, the greater the danger for the teen and the community in which she lives. A large parent/teen gulf aggravates serious risk-taking behavior in the "Big Four" risk domains: driving, drugs, sex and technology.

The argument ended badly. The young man flew out of the house in a rage, jumped into the car and zoomed backwards out of the driveway. Once in the street he accelerated rapidly, and by the time he approached the Smiths' yard, he was going over fifty miles per hour. Unfortunately, there was a curve in the road at that point which the young man couldn't negotiate. His car shot across the front yard and struck the three-year old. The frantic mother rushed over and picked up her daughter. As Mom looked down, the little girl's eyes rolled back in her head. She died in her mother's arms.

The girl would not have been killed if the sixteen-year old had not had the argument with his parents about his independence. And no, we certainly can't prevent all parent-adolescent arguments. But the fact of the matter is this: The more hostility and distance there is in our society between parents and teenagers, the more frequently adolescents will act out their negative feelings in activities involving driving, drugs and alcohol, sex and internet risks. It's happening every day. Recall our data on deaths and teen driving, adolescent experimentation with drugs, sexually transmitted diseases and teen pregnancy, and adolescent use of technology.

What to do? You need to use your appreciation of adolescence (Chapter 1) and knowledge of normal teen behavior (Chapter 2), combined with an understanding of your reactions to The Snub (Introduction) and teen risk-taking (Chapter 3), to come up with a new job description for yourself. Let's take a look at one in Chapter 5.

One thing is clear: The hostility/distance wall between parents and teens causes large amounts of suffering and injury—everyday—to adolescents as well as other innocent people. You don't want to help build the barrier.

Your New Job Description

Do these parents look like they're ready to check out a new job description for themselves. No. Why is that? It's because their fifteen-year old just walked out the door and only grunted when they said, "Have a nice day?" They're thinking, "So what are we, chopped liver?"

How are we going to deal with this couple? We're going to try to pull off a major *attitude adjustment* with them. The adjustment has to start with realistic sympathy for them: The Snub is unpleasant! But their teen's behavior is normal and it is not a sign that they (Mom and Dad) did anything wrong. Teens all over the world are treating their parents the same way: snubbing the older folks and scaring them. This behavior, however, doesn't mean the teens are screwy. Distancing themselves from parents is one way for the kids to manage a horrendously long, and insulting adolescence that wasn't their idea in the first place.

Parent of adolescent: The new job description and attitude adjustment will depend on some bad news and some good news. Let's plow through it.

The Bad News

The bad news has three parts. First of all, when your kids were little, you certainly worried about their behavior, but not as much as you do now. Why? The stakes seem to be higher at this point. It's drinking and driving now vs. the toddler who got out of bed then. It's sexual behavior now vs. not eating all her dinner then. Drug taking vs. sibling rivalry. And so on.

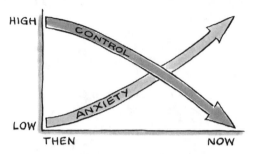

Second, while your anxiety level has risen due to the increased severity of the possible behavioral consequences, your control has dropped way down. When the toddler got out of bed, you were there to do something about it. When the youngster wouldn't eat her dinner, you were physically present and could come up with some way of dealing with the refusal. Now, however, it's different. The teens, if they want, can tailgate in the car. They can have sex if the opportunity presents itself, experiment with marijuana or access porn sites on the web. You can no longer physically stop them; you are no longer The Director.

Third, if you want to see things change, to the extent that you can still affect your kids' behavior, you will have to change first. The teens have too much on their plate, and they will not reach out to you.

The Good News

That's the bad news. Now the good news. First, most teens don't kill themselves or others while driving, get addicted to drugs, get pregnant

or get STDs, or have disastrous encounters with technology. Even if you did nothing intelligent about your relationship with your kids, odds are they would not be ruined by their behavior.

Second, research show that your differences with your kids are not as revolutionary as you might think. On the one hand, for example, it appears teens are more affected by their peers than by parents in matters such as dress, appearance, musical tastes, friendships and their treatment of adults. On the other hand, however, parents have more affect on an adolescent's basic life values, such as kindness, hard work, ability to follow the rules and cooperate with others, effort and courage. Parents also significantly affect a youngster's educational plans.

Third, in spite of their behavior, teens still care a lot about what their parents think of them and of how they're doing with the gigantic tasks involved in growing up. That's one of the sad things about parents doing The Resnub. Irritated, rejected moms and dads don't show appreciation or encouragement for a teenager's hard work. And yes, hard work (in fact, very hard work!) can involve something as straightforward as getting out of bed and showing up at school with a pimple the size of Mt. McKinley in the middle of your forehead.

> **DO YOU REMEMBER?**
>
> How much did it matter to you what your parents thought of you when you were an adolescent? What would you have told your friends if the issue ever came up? Did your parents give you much feedback about how they thought you were doing in terms of both strengths and weaknesses?

Finally in the good news category, research has repeatedly confirmed that teens do best and get hurt less frequently when parents a) maintain some reasonable type of behavioral monitoring and b) maintain as open and as friendly a relationship with the adolescents as possible, as opposed to a hostile and distant one. So, though

it isn't always possible (and yes, sometimes it is too late), our job description is geared toward these two goals.

The New Job Description

1. *Don't Take It Personally (Part II):* By and large, teens' aggravating behavior (rejection and risk) is not directed at you, their parent. This behavior, instead, is the result of adolescence itself. Understand that and your angry reaction will change.

2. *Manage and Let Go (Part III):* Teens may say they want you to totally leave them alone. Too bad. Some reasonable monitoring is still required, but you also need to know when to keep you mouth shut and let the kids handle their own lives.

3. *Stay in Touch (Part IV):* Once you've gotten the urge to Resnub out of your system, how do you relate to someone who won't answer a simple question like "How was your day?" First, you avoid the Four Cardinal Sins and second, you employ four simple connection building strategies.

4. *Take Care of Yourself (Part V):* If life isn't treating you too well, you're the last person in the world who should be trying to "manage" a worrisome teen. How do you know if your negative emotions come from the kid or from yourself? You don't, so you'd better deal with yourself first.

5. *Relax and Enjoy the Movie (Part VI):* Handle items 1-4 reasonably well and maybe you'll be able to calm down, let go and enjoy—most of the time, anyway—the unfolding of your adolescent's life.

Your primary goal is no longer to control your teens. Your goal is to help them become competent adults who leave home, establish new relationships, contribute something to the world and who enjoy life.

> *I hope you never fear those mountains in the distance*
> *Never settle for the path of least resistance*
> *Livin' might mean takin' chances, but they're worth takin'*
> *Lovin' might be a mistake, but it's worth makin'*
>
> — Lee Ann Womack, *I Hope You Dance*

To do your part you'll have to let go of your director role and ease into more of a consultant position. The teen's going to be doing most of the work, with the assistance, hopefully, of a positive relationship with you.

PART II

Don't Take It Personally

CHAPTER 6

Making Sense of The Snub

Yelling in my ear, you try to control me
Yelling in my ear, you look but you don't see.

– Operation Ivy, *Yelling My Ear*

The first step to not taking your teen's behavior personally is to understand The Snub. In the Introduction we observed an innocent Mom and Dad asking an innocent question of their sullen-looking son. As usual the conversation went nowhere, leaving everyone stymied and frustrated. In Chapter 4 we examined some of the parents' thoughts about the conversation—or lack thereof. Their thoughts, such as "What's wrong with him!?" and "How ungrateful!" made Mom and Dad feel angry and rejected.

Thoughts cause feelings. Your sister, for example, normally calls you every three days. But she hasn't called for a week. You might think "Did I say or do something wrong?" This thought would make you worried. Or you might think, "Why is she being so inconsiderate that she can't even give me a quick buzz, text or email?" This thought would make you irritated.

After eight days with no contact, however, you text her and find out her daughter—your niece—has had pneumonia and was in the hospital. Your sister was frantic with worry and running all over the place, so she never took the time to call. Your thoughts "Did I do something wrong?" and "Why is she so inconsiderate?" were both incorrect. Once you have better information (new thoughts), you think, "That's tough—the poor thing!" and you feel sympathetic and concerned for her.

Let's apply this formula to The Snub. When we ask parents at our *Surviving Your Adolescents* seminars—most of whom have been snubbed at some time or other by their teenagers—why the kids behave like this, the parents are often puzzled. They say things like, "It's just stupid," "There's no reason for it," "He's just being rude," " They just don't want to talk" or "She's too wrapped up in herself." These explanations aren't satisfying, though, and the parents still feel at a loss.

Decoding "Fine" and "Nothin'"

Believe it or not, we can explain The Snub, and that explanation should make you feel relieved. First of all, think back to being sixteen yourself. How did you feel when your parents asked you how your day was? There's a good possibility that a) you did not welcome this question and b) you felt the question was unnecessary and at least somewhat intrusive.

Why? Because you were an adolescent. *You wanted to handle life yourself,* and you didn't want to feel babied by your parents. You didn't feel you wanted to share all your private life with your mother and father. *Self-revelation was more and more for friends, not parents.* Who wanted to talk with Mom and Dad about friends, sex, romance, curiosity about smoking, or the embarrassing experience you just had in history class? Though you weren't able to leave home physically just yet, you sure as hell could leave home mentally.

In fact, teens tend to *translate* innocent-sounding parental questions. They often hear things that may or may not be intended. To an adolescent "How was your day?" can feel like "yelling in my ear"—even though it's not—and like an unwarranted attempt to pry and to control. Here, for instance, are some possible teen "translations" of the question "How was your day?"

PARENT SAYS...	TEEN'S TRANSLATION...
"HOW WAS YOUR DAY?"	"ARE YOU OK, DEAR?"
"HOW WAS YOUR DAY?"	"IT'S TIME FOR YOUR DAILY REPORT."
"HOW WAS YOUR DAY?"	"DID YOU SCREW UP ANYTHING TODAY THAT WE NEED TO KNOW ABOUT?"

The teen might like to say "Shut the hell up!" but he's too polite for that. So let's try to grasp the real meaning behind his words:

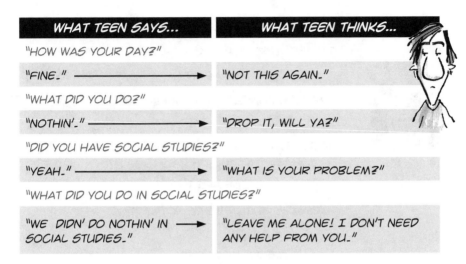

WHAT TEEN SAYS...	WHAT TEEN THINKS...
"HOW WAS YOUR DAY?"	
"FINE."	"NOT THIS AGAIN."
"WHAT DID YOU DO?"	
"NOTHIN'."	"DROP IT, WILL YA?"
"DID YOU HAVE SOCIAL STUDIES?"	
"YEAH."	"WHAT IS YOUR PROBLEM?"
"WHAT DID YOU DO IN SOCIAL STUDIES?"	
"WE DIDN' DO NOTHIN' IN SOCIAL STUDIES."	"LEAVE ME ALONE! I DON'T NEED ANY HELP FROM YOU."

As time goes on and frustration builds, the parents' question may actually take on a different meaning. Since they know they are going to get stonewalled, even though their words are the same, Mom and Dad may really be saying something else entirely:

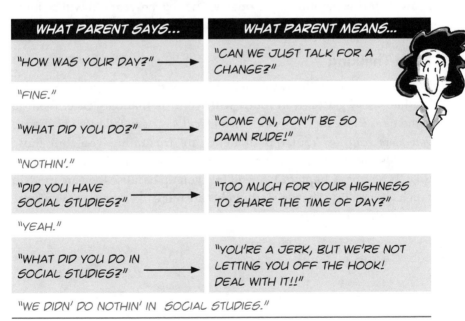

WHAT PARENT SAYS...	WHAT PARENT MEANS...
"HOW WAS YOUR DAY?"	"CAN WE JUST TALK FOR A CHANGE?"
"FINE."	
"WHAT DID YOU DO?"	"COME ON, DON'T BE SO DAMN RUDE!"
"NOTHIN'."	
"DID YOU HAVE SOCIAL STUDIES?"	"TOO MUCH FOR YOUR HIGHNESS TO SHARE THE TIME OF DAY?"
"YEAH."	
"WHAT DID YOU DO IN SOCIAL STUDIES?"	"YOU'RE A JERK, BUT WE'RE NOT LETTING YOU OFF THE HOOK! DEAL WITH IT!!"
"WE DIDN' DO NOTHIN' IN SOCIAL STUDIES."	

Putting the two "conversations" together, we get a better idea over time of what's really going on and what's really being said. It's not pretty.

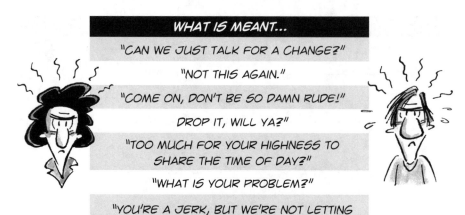

WHAT IS MEANT...

"CAN WE JUST TALK FOR A CHANGE?"

"NOT THIS AGAIN."

"COME ON, DON'T BE SO DAMN RUDE!"

DROP IT, WILL YA?"

"TOO MUCH FOR YOUR HIGHNESS TO SHARE THE TIME OF DAY?"

"WHAT IS YOUR PROBLEM?"

"YOU'RE A JERK, BUT WE'RE NOT LETTING YOU OFF THE HOOK! DEAL WITH IT!!"

"LEAVE ME ALONE! I DON'T NEED ANY HELP FROM YOU."

As the song said, "Go ahead with your own life, leave me alone." At this point everyone is frustrated—probably furious. The parents may show their exasperation more openly. The sixteen-year old will be more subtle; he may act sullen, but he will be boiling inside.

Hard Thinking

What's the solution? It's attitude adjustment time—for the parents, not the kid. First, get back in touch with your own adolescence, then do some hard thinking. *This hard thinking will make you feel better by making you more realistic.* Your old thoughts are frustrating you, but those thoughts are off-base. They are "garbage" thoughts. Newer thoughts (like those from Chapters 2–5) will free you up because they are more in touch with reality. The newer thoughts are more like "pearls of wisdom" because they *make more sense.*

GARBAGE THOUGHTS	NEW INSIGHTS
"WHAT'S WRONG WITH HIM!?" →	"NOTHING. HE'S A NORMAL SIXTEEN-YEAR OLD."
"WHAT DID WE DO WRONG?" →	"NOTHING. YOU'RE JUST CONCERNED PARENTS, BUT YOU NEED A DIFFERENT APPROACH. RELAX A LITTLE."
"BUT IT'S JUST A SIMPLE QUESTION!" →	"NO, IT'S COMPLEX. BECAUSE HE'S A TEEN, HE TAKES YOUR QUESTION AS PRYING."
"WHY IS SHE REJECTING ME?" →	"SHE'S NOT REJECTING YOU AS MUCH AS SHE IS THE IDEA OF PARENTAL ASSISTANCE; SHE WANTS TO BE ON HER OWN."
"CAN'T SHE BE A LITTLE NICER ABOUT IT?" →	"THAT WOULD BE NICE, BUT IT'S PROBABLY NOT GOING TO HAPPEN. IT'S AWKWARD FOR EVERYBODY."

Get your thoughts over to the righthand side. That's more realistic and it will feel better. Adolescence is tough—the kids don't quite know what to do with Mom and Dad anymore. You, the parent, are not really being rejected and you did not do anything wrong.

Don't Set Yourself Up

After listening to this analysis at the *Surviving Your Adolescents* seminar, parents often express the following concern: Well, if we can't even have a simple conversation, how are we supposed to stay in touch? First of all, you're certainly not staying in touch with the "How was your day?/ Fine" routine. Also think about it: Do you really need to be doing a daily diagnosis of how your kid's life is going? In Part IV we'll discuss some concrete ideas for how to stay in touch as much as possible. But until your adolescents reach adulthood, you're not likely to have the closeness you may have had in the past. Closeness is more for peers now.

The "How was your day?" dilemma brings up an interesting question. Why would a reasonable and well-meaning parent continually ask a question that not only gets nowhere but also causes trouble? The most common response from parents is that they just don't know what else to do. So they kind of stay on "automatic" and bullheadedly or naively go ahead with the same fruitless inquiry.

What other options are there? First, at all costs, don't ask that question in any form (if the question works, of course, no problem). By not asking that question, you will accomplish two feats: 1) you will not aggravate your teenager and 2) you will not set yourself up to feel rejected. Other alternatives? Start a conversation about crime, politics, sports or weather; if you get little or no response, just drop it or say—sympathetically, not judgmentally—"You don't feel much like talking tonight, do you? That's OK." If two parents are at the table, talk to each other and let the youngster join if she wants to. Another choice is to consider eating separately a few days a week. And finally, just don't say anything and see what happens! That may be uncomfortable, but it will certainly be entertaining!

"Yelling in my ear, you look but you don't see." You don't want your kids to feel you're yelling in their ear (even if you know you're not). And you do want to look across the dinner table and see that there's a different person there now. It's not your baby.

So that's what The Snub is all about and that's what the gloomy looking teen is thinking while he's busy snubbing. And you can do everyone a world of good if you work really hard to change the way you think. Some parents ask at this point, "Why should I have to be the one to change—he's almost an adult. What about his responsibility?"

It's a good question. First of all, changing your thinking should be done no matter what your kid does. Why? Because it's simply more realistic, and being more realistic will make you feel better. Appreciating how normal teens think—and how you thought way back when—is basically getting back in touch with reality. That's always a good idea.

Second, it is highly unlikely that your adolescent is going to give up this way of relating to you as long as he is living in your house. Things will change later, but not now. So you have a choice: You can waste your time being angry with a kid for being a normal teen, or you can relax, not take it personally, and allow your son or daughter to do the same thing you did when you were their age.

ATTITUDE ADJUSTMENT

CHAPTER 7

"Don't Take It Personally" in Action

Now that we've made sense of The Snub and you have a better understanding (and recall) of what adolescence is about, we're ready to apply that knowledge to making you feel better and to getting along better with your teen. This will make your youngster less likely to get hurt, but it's also just a more pleasant way to live for the whole family.

In this chapter we're going to examine closely two incidents that involve a) typical but difficult adolescent behavior and b) the normal irritated reactions of parents. You recall from Chapter 5 that irritated, worried and rejected parents often do the following: Resnub, make irritable comments, become bad listeners, get very uncreative and try to exercise control that they don't have.

Here we'll look at two of these parental reactions, The Resnub and bad listening. The procedure for "not taking it personally" involves four basic steps. These steps are as follows:

1. Take responsibility for the problem.
2. Stop and think.
3. Move from garbage thoughts to realistic thoughts.
4. Act according to your new ideas.

Here we go.

The Resnub: Taking It Personally

One form The Snub takes is the kids' not wanting to go out in public with you. Let's play the scene through the *bad* way first. Dad says to fifteen-year-old daughter:

Dad thinks the following:

As a consequence of these thoughts, Dad is angry. As a consequence of being angry, Dad blurts out:

The results: 1) The hostility / distance wall between child and parents gets higher, 2) the adolescent is less safe to herself and her community, and 3) it's a lousy way for this family to live.

The Resnub: Take 2

Now let's do a "Take 2" on this scene and have Dad use our four steps. Maybe Dad shouldn't even ask the question, but let's assume he still does:

Step 1: Dad starts to get miffed, but then he tells himself: "She's just being herself and she's not going to change. In the interests of everybody, including myself, I've got to change."

Step 2: Dad takes a deep breath and stops to think. "Instead of being rigid and uncreative, I'm going to do something different," he says to himself.

Step 3: Dad reevaluates his usual line of thought and replaces old, unrealistic ideas with newer, more sensible ones. Like this:

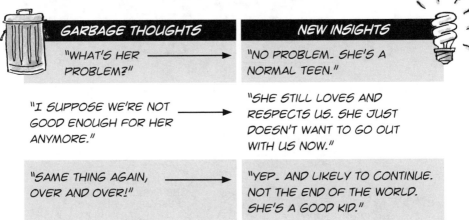

GARBAGE THOUGHTS	NEW INSIGHTS
"WHAT'S HER PROBLEM?"	"NO PROBLEM. SHE'S A NORMAL TEEN."
"I SUPPOSE WE'RE NOT GOOD ENOUGH FOR HER ANYMORE."	"SHE STILL LOVES AND RESPECTS US. SHE JUST DOESN'T WANT TO GO OUT WITH US NOW."
"SAME THING AGAIN, OVER AND OVER!"	"YEP. AND LIKELY TO CONTINUE. NOT THE END OF THE WORLD. SHE'S A GOOD KID."

Step 4: These new ideas do not cause problematic feelings. Dad acts according to the new thoughts and says:

The results: 1) The hostility/distance wall between child and parents lowered a bit, 2) the adolescent remains safe to herself and her community, and 3) this is a pleasant way for this family to live.

Listening: Wrong Way

Parents that feel irritated, rejected and worried can also become poor and biased listeners. When Mom picks him up after school, seventeen-year-old Ben, who hasn't been so easy to live with the last few years, gets in the car and says:

Mom thinks the following:

As a consequence of these thoughts, Mom is angry. As a consequence of being angry, Mom blurts out:

Both people fume silently.

Results: 1) The hostility/distance wall between Ben and Mom gets higher, 2) Ben is less safe to himself and the community, and 3) this is a lousy way for this family to live.

Listening: Right Way

Time for Take 2 on this scene—this time with Mom using our four steps. Ben says:

Step 1: Mom starts to get cranked, then she tells herself: "That's Ben and he's not going to change. In the interests of everybody, including myself, I've got to change. He also sounds more upset than usual."

Step 2: Mom takes a deep breath and stops to think, "Instead of being unsympathetic and inflexible, I'm going to do something different. "I'm going to try to find out what happened."

Step 3: Mom reevaluates her usual line of thought and replaces old, impracticable ideas with newer, more functional ones. Like this:

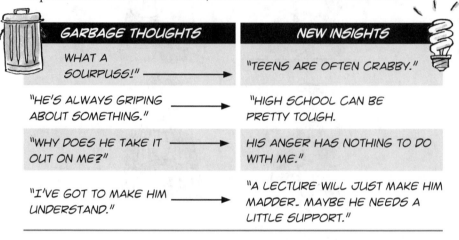

GARBAGE THOUGHTS	NEW INSIGHTS
WHAT A SOURPUSS!"	"TEENS ARE OFTEN CRABBY."
"HE'S ALWAYS GRIPING ABOUT SOMETHING."	"HIGH SCHOOL CAN BE PRETTY TOUGH.
"WHY DOES HE TAKE IT OUT ON ME?"	HIS ANGER HAS NOTHING TO DO WITH ME."
"I'VE GOT TO MAKE HIM UNDERSTAND."	"A LECTURE WILL JUST MAKE HIM MADDER. MAYBE HE NEEDS A LITTLE SUPPORT."

Step 4: These new ideas do not cause any extra unpleasant feelings. Mom acts according to the new thoughts and says:

The results: 1) The hostility/distance wall shrunk a little, 2) the adolescent is safer to himself and the community than he would have been if an argument between him and Mom had followed, and 3) this is a more pleasant way for this family to live.

Insight Plus Skill

Not taking your teen's behavior personally is both an insight and a skill. The insight has to do with appreciating the fact that adolescents rebel against adult supervision and authority, not necessarily against individual people. The insight also has to do with remembering that the teen years are stressful, confusing and aggravating—and long.

The skill has to do with practicing the four steps just described. You'll have good days and bad. But for the sake of yourself, your whole family and your teens, it's essential that you take charge of your own thoughts and feelings, trash your screwy reactions, and get back in touch with reality. Takes a while to get the hang of it!

HOW NOT TO TAKE IT PERSONALLY

1. TAKE RESPONSIBILITY FOR THE PROBLEM.

2. STOP AND THINK.

3. MOVE FROM GARBAGE TO INSIGHT THOUGHTS.

4. ACT ACCORDING TO YOUR NEW IDEAS.

PART III

Manage & Let Go

CHAPTER 8

Six Kids: Intervention Examples

In the next two parts of the book, we'll examine the art of managing and letting go of your teens and also the art of staying in touch with them as best you can. To understand these tasks, examples will help. So here are six kids whose problems range from the trivial to the sublime. In just a bit we'll come up with a parenting solution for each of them.

Chatty Cathy

Cathy is your fourteen-year-old daughter. She loves school and actually does pretty well in it. And she's got a ton of friends. The problem you have with her is that she seems to spend all night, every night it seems talking on the telephone. The conversations go something like this:

"Did you hear what happened in the cafeteria today? You didn't!? Oh, my god. OK, here's the deal. Well, Steve walked in the cafeteria with Linda, you know, they went out with each other for about six months and then they broke up…"

You're concerned about her school work, about her wasting time and about the phone bill. What are you going to do with Chatty Cathy?

Phinicky Phil

Phil is your seventeen-year-old son and he's a very good student. He's got a 3.85 grade point average on a four-point system. The problem you're having with him is that this semester he is flunking political science.

"Do you believe that dorkface is giving me an F in poly sci?"

"What!? I thought all your grades were great."

"Not with this jerk. El Bozo thinks he's God's gift to humanity. I mean, he's a complete nerd."

"I've never heard you talk like that before."

Phil says he can't work for this guy because he thinks the teacher is a jerk. What is going to be done with Phinicky Phil?

Silent Sue

Sue is a fifteen-year-old girl who used to be close to you. You used to talk a lot. But since the summer she's got a bunch of new friends. She doesn't come around as much as before and she's not at home as much. Her grades are a little lower and her dress is a little bit sloppier. And sometimes in addition to being distant she seems to be downright hostile. You're in the kitchen and Sue walks in.

"Hi—how's it going?"

"Great."

Sue leaves without saying another word. What are you going to do with Silent Sue?

Puffing Penny

Penny is a fifteen-year-old girl and she's smoking in her room for apparently the last few months. You know she's smoking in her room because you smell the smoke and the windows are sometimes left open. Another concern you have is this: Is she using cigarettes to cover the smell of marijuana? Penny has a C+ average in school and enjoys going out with her friends. You have sometimes wondered if any of them are using drugs, but you have no hard evidence for this. What are we going to do with Puffing Penny?

Crabby Carl

Carl is your sixteen-year-old son. After breaking up with his girlfriend a couple of months ago, Carl seems more irritable and distant. He has lost interest in TV, computer and homework. His grades have dropped some and he has uncharacteristically missed work a couple of times. Carl has trouble going to sleep at night and seems suddenly very self-critical. What are you going to do with Crabby Carl?

Obnoxious Arnie

Arnie is a nineteen-and-one-half-year-old lad who is still living at home. He graduated high school, but by the skin of his teeth. He is neither working nor going to school. Arnie uses the car, but puts no gas in it.

"Hey, did you use the car?"

"Yeah."

"Then how come there's no gas in it?"

"There's gas in it?"

"Oh yeah? Wanna know how empty that tank is? I could throw a match in there and nothing would happen."

"I'd like to see you try it."

"OK, wise guy, you're gonna take this car and put some gas in it. All the way up to full, you understand?"

Arnie is argumentative with his parents and sometimes verbally and physically abusive to siblings. He borrows money from others and sometimes steals it, but he does not pay anything back. He sleeps most of the day but stays up all night running up substantial bills for 900-number sex-line phone calls. Arnie refuses to see a counselor. What is going to be done with Obnoxious Arnie?

DO YOU REMEMBER?

If we had a seventh entry here, and the entry were to describe you as a teenager, how would the description read if you wrote it? How would it read if your parents had written it back then? Would your parents have wanted to change something about you?

CHAPTER 9

Establish House Rules

"I don't want you to tell me it's time to come home." Everyone is familiar with Billy Joel's plea (or demand). In a way, he has a point, and in another way, he's off base. He is correct in that adolescents' ferocious desire to run their own lives should be respected. He is wrong if he's saying there should no rules at all for teens. There will be House Rules of some kind until the kids leave home, whether that departure occurs at age eighteen or age twenty-five.

House rules should be maintained according to the following guidelines:

1. Rules should be minimal.
2. Rules should be clear and understood the same by everyone.
3. Unless they are dreadful, first offenses should be calmly and briefly discussed but not punished.
4. Rules may change as teens get older and more competent.

In this chapter we'll talk about how to set up and maintain rules in general and how to deal with repeated offenses. Check out the Appendix for suggestions on how to handle less earthshaking issues such as bedtime, homework, parties, grades, sibling rivalry, swearing and chores.

Setting Up and Maintaining Rules

No teen is going to be especially fond of anything that smacks of parental authority. So it's best if the process of setting up and maintaining rules is done as quickly and painlessly as possible. It's also important to keep in mind that the kind of relationship you have with the kids will greatly affect their response to any rules you want to establish. The basic idea is something like this:

> **RULES + RELATIONSHIP = DISCIPLINE**
>
> **RULES − RELATIONSHIP = REBELLION**

The better your connection with your teenager, the easier it will be to implement rules. That means before you do much rule-oriented work, you should understand how not to take it personally (Part II), when to keep your mouth shut (Ch. 11), how to avoid the Four Cardinal Sins (Ch. 13), and how to stay in touch reasonably well (Part IV).

With the exception of the Big Four Risks, in many instances you won't need a lot of discussion about rules. If you're not having any particular problems with things like hours, homework, bedtime, money or meals, give everyone a pat on the back and enjoy the peace and quiet.

Two indicators will tell you that it's time to do something more. The first is *regular arguments* about a particular issue and the second is a *significant first offense* of some kind. With regard to hours, for example, if you and the teens are always arguing about what time they get home on the weekends, or if one of the kids all of a sudden comes home two hours late, it's time to sit down and write out an agreement about what the rules are and about what the consequences for violations will be.

Repeated Offenses

When adolescents repeat the same misbehavior, it's easy to get so irritated that you can hardly think straight. When the teen does something right, on the other hand, you may ignore the good deed and think, "Well, it's about time!" This defensive and aggressive stance on your part runs the risk of making the child so angry that he is more likely to engage in vengeful and hostile—as well as perhaps thrill-seeking— behavior. This reaction/counter reaction sequence can be the start of a domestic war, with the result that your child's safety and future are in great jeopardy. The Snub and The Resnub will be active.

Instead of engaging in angry, unproductive, knee-jerk parenting, your strategy with repeated problems should involve two primary lines of attack: 1) improving your relationship with your teenager through regular doses of praise, one-on-one shared fun, active listening and avoidance of the Four Cardinal Sins, and 2) close-but-reasonable supervision using your House Rules along with the what we call the Major/Minor System.

We'll discuss how to improve a relationship with a child more specifically in Part IV. Here we'll focus on the Major/Minor System. If problems recur, what you'll do, either in collaboration with your adolescent or by yourself (if she won't cooperate), is set up a well-defined system of behavioral consequences. The consequences or punishments will depend on the seriousness of the behavior involved, varying from major offenses to minor transgressions. Actually, it's usually helpful to have a three-level, Major/Medium/Minor list of consequences that include variations of groundings, fines, chores, community service or educational activities. For example:

Major Consequences (choose one)

Grounding: two weeks restriction to room after dinner and on weekends; no electronic entertainment (TV, computer, games) or phone

Fine: $50 or pay back double the value of stolen or damaged articles

Chores: 15 hours work around the house

Community service: 15 hours volunteer work at church or other institution

Educational activity: research subject (e.g., smoking) and write good-quality eight-page paper, attend group counseling

Medium Consequences (choose one)

Grounding: one-week restriction to room after dinner and on weekends; no electronic entertainment (TV, computer, games) or phone

Fine: $25 or pay back double the value of stolen or damaged articles

Chores: eight hours work around the house

Community service: eight hours volunteer work at church or other institution

Educational activity: research subject (e.g., smoking) and write good-quality four-page paper

Minor Consequences (choose one)

Grounding: two-day restriction to room after dinner; no electronic
entertainment (TV, computer, games) or phone
Fine: $10 or pay back double the value of stolen or damaged articles
Chores: four hours work around the house
Community service: four hours volunteer work at church or other
institution
Educational activity: research subject (e.g., smoking) and write
good-quality two-page paper

Make your own Major/Minor System, if you like, or borrow parts
from the one here. It's a good idea to write the thing out and have everyone sign the contract.

As you can see, the punishments for Major offenses are greater than
the punishments for Medium ones, and Medium consequences are bigger than those for Minor offenses. The above ideas are only suggestions:
These guidelines will certainly be altered by individual families. (Over
the years I have learned that *there will always be* some people who think
I am too strict, and others who think I am not strict enough!)

QUIK TIP

When a misbehavior
occurs, only one
consequence is
implemented after the
behavior is classified.
This saves a lot of effort
and lot of arguing, and
it lets your teen know
what the deal is
beforehand.

Once you have come up with your punishment
classifications, you (or you and your teen together)
decide which behavior merits which class of punishment. When that misbehavior occurs, *one* of the
consequences from the list is implemented (not
the whole list!). This process saves a lot of effort
and deliberation, and also lets your youngster
know the consequences beforehand if he decides
to mess up. Some parents even let the teenager
pick the consequence—once the parent has in-
voked the Major, Medium or Minor category.

Once the system is set up, when your adolescent repeats an offense, you simply categorize it
and determine the consequence. No yelling or screaming by you is allowed, of course, though a *short* explanation or discussion may occasionally be in order. Though it's tough to stay calm, especially when bad
behavior recurs, it is critical. Why? Simple: *Angry outbursts of righteous
indignation from parents obliterate the effectiveness of any punishments.* What
you'll have on your hands instead is a war.

What if the youngster does something that you didn't put on the original Major/Minor list? You just classify it as Major, Medium or Minor and then pick a punishment. You can adjust the Major/Minor System after you set it up, but be careful not to make punishments so harsh that they backfire. Remember that the Major/Minor System is intended to be a control on you as well as on your teen.

CAUTION

Angry outbursts, lectures or nagging are guaranteed to ruin the effects of any punishments you give out. Teens don't like parental authority in the first place! Keep working on your feelings about rejection and risk.

When setting up the Major/Minor System— and especially when imposing consequences—be prepared for certain predictable statements from your kids:

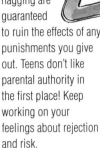

1. "This is stupid."
2. "I don't care what you do to me."
3. "My friends think you guys are weird."
4. "How come you don't treat anyone else around here like this?"

Don't pay any attention to these comments, but also don't smirk or act superior when the kids make them. Ninety per cent of the adolescents who say "I don't care" do care. Just be quiet, do what you have to do, and be prepared for some testing and manipulation.

If the Major/Minor System doesn't work, or you just can't seem to shut up, or you feel totally powerless, it may be time for professional evaluation and counseling.

What if, even if things are currently going swimmingly, you prefer to have rules in place for a number of potential problems? That's fine. Look at the next chapter for some ideas on managing the Big Four Risks and check the Appendix for thoughts on other problems.

AN EXAMPLE: RULES FOR GOING OUT

1. LET US KNOW WHERE YOU'RE GOING AND WHOM YOU'LL BE WITH.

2. UNDERSTAND WHAT TIME YOU NEED TO BE BACK.

3. CALL OR TEXT IF YOUR PLANS CHANGE.

4. HAVE A GOOD TIME!

CHAPTER 10

Managing the Big Four Risks

Every parent has worried thousands of times about her children get-ting hurt. Unfortunately, as much as you might like to you can't lock your kid in his bedroom and have him escorted to and from school by the police every day. One hundred percent control is not possible. What you want to do is to make sure you have taken reasonable steps for pre-venting injury to your kids by setting up House Rules, trying to stay in touch with the teens and taking care of yourself. Then you trust the youngsters to do their best.

There is a big difference between worry and preparation. Worrying may certainly lead to realistic planning, but good plans only need to be thought out and made once. Worry tends to go on and on and on, even long after good planning is finished. In other words, you may have taken perfectly good steps for preventing adolescent injury, but still find yourself worrying like crazy. For parents of teens, unfortunately, there's nothing unusual about that.

In this chapter we'll discuss some ideas for preventing injury from driving, drug or alcohol use, sex and romance and technology. There is nothing sacred about these suggestions, but many parents have found them useful. Keep in mind that your best preventive strategy is reasonable monitoring and maintaining as friendly and open a relationship as you can with your teenager.

Each of the next four chapter sections contains three parts:

1. Suggestions for preventing problems
2. Google information searches
3. Suggestions for handling problems if they occur

Part two, information searches, is educational. When parents say it's time to talk about drugs or sex, teens will often respond, "Oh, Mom, I already know about that stuff." A parent's response should be this: "Well, maybe you do, so maybe my job isn't to teach it to you. But my job is to make sure you have the facts. I don't know it all myself anyway, so here's what we'll do." The Google searches (for the first three risks) are an educational exercise you and your adolescent can do together. Take the ten searches we suggest (or make up your own) and have your teenager divide them up—five for her and five for you. Next, each of you do your research and come up with a brief Wikipedia-like summary of the topic. Then get together and share your information with each other. Try to listen, rather than teach, lecture or instruct. Your kids do know a lot of this stuff already.

Driving: Problem Prevention

Without being haughty, explain to your kids that their use of your car, other than for necessities like school, is a privilege. It's *your* car and you are letting them use it; they don't have an inherent right to your automobile.

Try to model good driving habits for your kids from the time they are little. Especially avoid speeding, tailgating, forgetting the seatbelt and drinking and driving. In addition to the training received at school, it's a good idea for each child to drive a total of 1,000 miles with her parents before getting her license. For this practice, include all kinds of conditions, such as driving in residential areas, on expressways, and in good and bad weather. You can even make an outing of the practice session and perhaps have some fun together! The teen keeps track of the miles logged; you get a feel for how competent she is behind the wheel.

Consider having your adolescent pay part or all of his insurance, and before he can start driving, he must have six months' worth of insurance payments in the bank. He can't drive without a parent—even if he has his license—until that money is saved. After that he pays you his portion of the insurance one month at a time. If your adolescent qualifies for the good-student insurance discount (usually twenty-five percent), that amount is taken off what he has to pay for his insurance because he earned it.

Teens should pay for their own gas; don't give them your credit card. If you agree to allow a competent adolescent to get his own car, he foots the bill. Make sure House Rules about issues like grades and hours are clear. If the kid does accomplish the feat of getting his own wheels, however, recognize the accomplishment. It's a thrill for him! Don't let your anxiety rain on his parade.

Your policy will be zero tolerance for drinking and driving. If the kid has one beer, he can't drive. If your adolescent has had something to drink, he or she must find a designated driver, call a cab or call you for a ride. If the teen calls under these circumstances, make sure not to berate him. No other teen, however, may regularly drive your family car. Cell phone usage in the car by teens younger than sixteen-and-a-half will be prohibited, except in emergencies. Your state may also prohibit sixteen-year-olds

> **NOTE...**
> Using your car is a privilege. It's *your* car and you are letting them use it; they don't have an inherent right to your automobile.

from driving between 9 p.m. and 5 a.m. for the first six months, except for work or school activities. Also for the first six months, a driver can only carry one passenger under the age of nineteen outside of her immediate family. Front and back seat seatbelts must be worn at all times. Violations of these rules will be considered medium to major offenses.

Google Searches

- Aggressive Driving
- GDL Laws
- Drug Impaired Driving
- Cell Phones and Driving
- Texting and Driving
- Road Rage (not Aggressive Driving)

- Work Zone Traffic Laws
- Teenage Driver Crash Statistics
- High-Risk Driving Situations
- Passenger Restrictions for
  New drivers

Driving: Managing Problems

Consider a setup with your adolescent that combines the GDL laws of your state with our Major/Minor System, where consequences for misbehavior consist of temporary groundings of different lengths of time from use of the car. It's a good idea to write out and sign this agreement in advance—you might save a few lives. Punishable offenses might include accidents and/or tickets due to reckless or careless driving, cell phone use or texting, or having too many passengers in the car. For example, a ticket for going ten miles over the speed limit might be a two-week restriction. An exception will not be made for driving to work or school, even though this may cause considerable inconvenience for other family members. When kids can still drive to work or school, "side trips" become inevitable, dilute the effect of the consequence, and cause many arguments.

> **NOTE...**
> Drinking and driving will be treated as a major offense. The consequence will be a six month to one year grounding from the car.

Second episodes of accidents or tickets will escalate the Major/Minor consequences. These consequences might involve not only grounding, but also driving lessons that the teen pays for. The driving instructor is asked to teach the child defensive driving, and the teen cannot drive again until at least three lessons have been completed and the instructor says the adolescent is ready.

Drinking and driving, whether or not an accident or ticket is involved, will be followed by a minimum six-month-to-one-year grounding from the car. Community service of some kind may be used to work off not more than twenty-five percent of the restriction period.

Drugs and Alcohol: Problem Prevention

Do your best not to model drug and alcohol use. Evaluate and define your own attitudes toward these activities. If you have an addiction to something, like smoking or drinking, admit it to your kids, tell them how you got the problem, and say that—even though you're trying—it's a hard habit to beat.

When the child is younger, consider educational activities such as your daughter's volunteering at or visiting a drug/alcohol rehab center for a while. Ask your kids what they know or have learned at school or elsewhere about alcohol and drug use. Listen carefully, ask good questions and don't get into lecturing. Don't feel like you have to know everything (like all the street names for all the drugs), because first of all, you can't, and second of all, the drug scene is changing all the time.

When you hear of a drug- or alcohol-related tragedy, don't take the opportunity to lecture your kids about the dangers involved. Drawing obvious conclusions or using scare tactics is not helpful with adolescents. Instead, see what your children have to say about the tragedy, try to ask intelligent, probing questions and listen carefully to their thoughts.

> **NOTE...**
> If your teen is going out, make sure the rules are clear but don't repeat this information every time. Make sure the last thing out of your mouth as the adolescent leaves is "Have a good time."

Don't leave your teens home by themselves overnight. If you are going out in the evening and your teens are going to be home by themselves, ask them what they would do if some other kids dropped by who had been drinking and who wanted to continue to party at your house. Make sure your children have some idea what to say, as well as what to do if calling a neighbor or the police becomes necessary.

If your teen is going out, make sure the rules about hours are clear. Don't repeat this information every time he walks out the door, however. If hours are already understood, simply tell him to have a good time. If you feel there is legitimate cause for concern, wait up for him. Otherwise, go to bed.

Google Searches

- THC
- Inhalants
- Drug Dependence
- AIDS and Drug Use
- Drugs, Alcohol and Pregnancy
- Stimulants
- Depressants
- Alcohol Abuse Facts
- Drugs and Peers
- Heroin and LSD

Drugs and Alcohol: Managing Problems

Drug and alcohol problems, obviously, are best dealt with early, so don't waste time if you feel there is cause for concern. Drug abuse in its advanced stages is extremely difficult to turn around. If you suspect there is a problem, you may want to contact your local health department or a nearby hospital and talk to a drug/alcohol counselor about your worries and what to do.

Signs that drug use is a problem include the following:

- unusual mood swings
- change of friends
- suddenly falling grades

- increased irritability
- withdrawal
- sudden secretiveness
- being obviously under the influence
- going through substantial amounts of money with nothing to show for it

If your teen comes in late at night and obviously under the influence, acknowledge that there is a problem *but don't talk about it then.* The next morning make an appointment to talk as soon as possible. Your family doctor or a psychiatrist can leave a standing order at an emergency room or the doctor's office for a drug urinalysis. The order should say that the test will be "surveilled," i.e., someone will watch the teen produce the urine. Such tests can be useful as part of psychological treatment, or they may tell you that it's time to get psychological treatment. The best time to have the test done? First thing in the morning after a night of suspicious activities. Calmly tell the teen that refusal to do the test means to you that the results would have been positive.

NOTE...
If you are worried about drug use, but have reason to believe that only mild experimentation has occurred, consider having the child attend an AODA program at an outpatient facility.

If you are worried about drug or alcohol use but have good reason to believe that only minor experimentation has been involved, have the child attend an educational program given by an outpatient AODA (alcohol and other drug abuse) clinic, health department or local hospital. Monitor urine for a few months afterwards. Don't feel you have to either be the local drug expert or that you have to know more than your teenager about drugs. You'll make things a lot worse if you act like you know what you're talking about when you really don't.

What about your kids drinking with you at your house? A sample of wine or a beer for special occasions or toasts is fine. Regular, recreational drinking with you is not.

 ## Sex and Romance: Problem Prevention

The best way to discuss sex is gradually and frequently as the kids grow up, as questions arise and as the topic pops up in daily life. Ideally, sex should be discussed in a way children can understand at their age.

If you have been doing that, that's great and keep it up. Unfortunately, this lovely idea doesn't get implemented very often. Kids don't spontaneously ask sex-related questions, and parents rarely take the opportunity to explain something when an issue does "pop up." Our society may be sexually overstimulated, but we certainly aren't comfortable talking openly about anything even remotely related to human reproduction or sexual feelings.

To make matters worse, when parents think about the sex education of their children, they always seem to come up with this funny idea of "The Big Talk." This notion implies some kind of know-it-all parent imparting useful sexual information to a receptive child who can hardly wait to get the real scoop. Closer to the truth is this: On the one hand, we have an anxious parent with imperfect knowledge and a vague idea of where to begin who dreads the idea of talking to his teenage son. On the other hand, we have a teenage son who finds the thought of his parent talking about sex disgusting, and who, quite defensively, thinks he knows all that is necessary anyway.

> **NOTE...**
> Unfortunately, we often have a fifteen-year-old kid who thinks that the idea of his parent talking about sex is disgusting and who also believes he knows all there is to know anyway.

So what are you going to do? Here are a few thoughts: Don't feel guilty if you get the creeps even thinking about discussing sex with your child. Also, keep in mind that whatever the kids may or may not have actually done sexually, few teens are going to think of themselves as novices as far as sexual knowledge goes. They've been exposed to different information from school, friends, movies and TV, as well as from books and magazines. They may feel—rightly or wrongly—that they're quite well informed. No adolescent wants to see himself or herself as sexually naïve.

If you say to your teen, "Sometime you and I have to discuss sex," and you are met with, "Mom, I already know about all that stuff!" here are a few ideas. First of all, define "all that stuff." All that stuff arguably falls into four categories: a) the biomechanics of pregnancy, b) the biomechanics of sexually transmitted diseases, c) the connection between sex and romance, and d) sexual values. Consider discussing the following:

Google Searches
- Ovulation Calendar
- Chlamydia and Gonorrhea
- Date Rape
- AIDS Transmission

- Sexual Intercourse
- Men and Romance
- Gay Teens
- Limerence

- Condoms, The Pill and "Morning After" Drugs
- Sexual Abstinence

Another sometimes-more-entertaining way of breaking down sex-talk barriers is to discuss with your teenager some of the common sex myths. **Can you, for example, explain where the following statements might have come from and why they are incorrect?**

- ⊘ You can't get pregnant if you have sex standing up.
- ⊘ You can't get pregnant the first time you have intercourse.
- ⊘ Oral sex is a good way to prevent STDs.
- ⊘ Condoms are always reliable.
- ⊘ Most teenagers are having casual sex.
- ⊘ Contraception is the responsibility of the female.
- ⊘ You can't get pregnant during your period.
- ⊘ If someone has an STD infection, you can tell by looking at them.
- ⊘ All STDs can be cured.
- ⊘ There's no good way to determine if you're ready to have sex.

Here's another alternative. You explain to your adolescent, "Look. My job may not be to give you all the information about sex. It may be more just to make sure you know it so you don't get hurt. I'm talking about things like getting pregnant (or getting someone else pregnant), forced sex and sexually transmitted diseases like gonorrhea and gruesome things like that. Let's do this. I'm going to make up ten sex questions for you, and I want you to make up ten for me. You can try to stump me if you want, but I can try and stump you too. Then we sit down a few times and throw the questions at each other. Of course, we make sure we come up with the right answers. Then you're free to pursue your own existence with no more hassles from me. How about it?" Once again, don't feel like you have to be the resident sex expert in your house. Your teen will find it refreshing if you honestly acknowledge that you don't know everything about the subject.

You recall our discussion earlier regarding the connection between an open and friendly parent/teen relationship and the teen's being less likely to get hurt? One research study looked at teens who had good relationships with their parents and teens who had bad relationships.

Then the researchers got information about the sexual activity of these kids. There was, in a sense, good news and bad news. Contrary to what you might hope, the adolescents with good relationships were just as sexually active as the adolescents with poor relationships. The good news, though, was that the kids with good relationships were more likely to use birth control to protect themselves from pregnancy and STDs.

Sex and Romance: Managing Problems

If you are worried about STDs and have an open relationship with your son or daughter, you might ask him if he thinks he needs a checkup. Where a relationship is less candid, other parents simply ask their family doctor to do the appropriate tests for sexually transmitted diseases, without the teen knowing it, the next time the child has a physical. If the results are positive, perhaps the doctor, the adolescent and you can discuss it together.

If you are worried about sexual abuse, you may ask the sensitive questions, "Has anyone ever made unwanted or forced sexual advances to you?" and "Would you tell me if they had?" Keep in mind that many kids who have been abused still won't admit it. If the child admits that something has happened, it's time for them to see a therapist who has experience with this kind of problem. As a parent, you may be so upset that you need to talk to someone yourself. Always take seriously any child's statements or hints that she has been abused by someone. The worst thing to do is to scold her for making ridiculous claims. You'll never hear from her again on this subject and the abuse may continue.

> **NOTE...**
>
> "Look. My job may not be to give you all the information about sex. It may be more just to make sure you know it so you don't get hurt. I'm talking about things like getting pregnant (or getting someone else pregnant), forced sex and sexually transmitted diseases like gonorrhea and gruesome things like that."

Your daughter tells you she's pregnant. What should you do first? Maybe you should first listen again to Madonna's *Pappa Don't Preach*. Then you make sure you do no harm. You and your girl will forever remember your immediate response. You will be shocked and horrified, but you can rest assured that your daughter is in worse shape. Give her a hug. Cry if you feel like it. Ask a few questions, but no temper tantrums or "I told you so!" If you're so upset you can't see straight, wait a few hours before you try to talk. If your spouse goes ballistic, get him or her away.

Next, contact a pregnancy counseling service. Find one that provides actual counseling and not merely abortion screening. Your daughter will need someone to talk to other than you about what to do, and she needs to evaluate her three alternatives: adoption, abortion or keeping the baby. Large numbers of young girls opt for abortion or choose to keep the baby. Far fewer put their babies up for adoption.

If your teenage son is going to be a father: in few situations will the relationship between the two adolescents last. Ask your son how he's going to manage the situation, how he can support the girl, and how the decision will be made about the baby. Ask him what you can do to help.

Technology: Problem Prevention

Kids' daily consumption of mass communication by means of various tech devices gets larger and larger every year (so does their parents'). Recent estimates tell us that over 7.5 hours per day are spent by 8–18 year olds with TV, cell phones, music, computer, video games, print and movies. Some people claim the real figure should be 10.5 hours, because about three of the daily techcom hours are spent "multitasking," which means doing two or more things (TV, texting, surfing) at the same time.

Technology, in fact, is no longer controllable. But our discussion is not meant to scare you away from all the new techcom gadgetry. Liken your child's use of technology to driving a car. Driving a car is serious business. No competent parent would allow their child to drive without some instruction and agreement on the vehicle's use.

It may seem overwhelming, but let's look at some fairly simple guidelines for making technology a positive part of your family's life. First of all, you're going to have to talk with the kids and develop some guidelines for techcom use. In doing this you'll need some of the skills and attitudes we will discuss in Chapters 14.

Second, you're going to have to know what to talk about. Below you'll find a list of some of the most important issues you'll want to cover. As you carry on these one-on-one or family meetings, keep this in mind: With teens bring up the issue, then listen first to what they have to say. With many tech issues, the kids will have more to teach you than vice versa, so be humble and listen! Discuss, ask questions, then formulate your agreements. Signed contracts are a good idea. Below are the issues you'll want to clarify.

TechCom Selection and Setup

1. Before purchase, the capabilities of each device will be understood.
2. Computers will be kept in public places: not in the bedroom.
3. Consider installing monitoring software; monitoring software keeps a record of what your child does on the computer.
4. Install filtering software for Internet use; though they are not perfect, filters help block inappropriate sites.
5. Deactivate the online component of techcom gadgets with Internet capabilities that can't be filtered.
6. Set all privacy settings, especially on social networks, to their highest level.

TechCom Input to Your Home

1. Teach your children not to open unexpected emails or spam links, which may lead to porn sites or computer viruses.
2. Check ratings for video games, TV shows, and movies.
3. Include your specific time constraints for techcom use. For example, "Two hours techplay after homework is done."
4. Clarify exactly which websites, movies or games are off limits.
5. Don't leave your own Internet-accessible devices lying around.

TechCom Outputs from Your Kids

1. Discuss not giving out personal information online, such as last name, address, school names, pictures, etc.
2. Discuss not giving out passwords to anyone or changing computer settings without your permission.
3. Discuss meeting online friends in person; agree to accompany them to any first meeting.
4. Establish rules for gossip or cyberbullying.
5. Tell your children what to do if a pornographic image comes up; for example, turn off screen and find a parent.
6. Discuss filesharing with the kids. Some file sharing is illegal, and some filesharing programs can "share" other private files from your computer that you don't want shared.

TechCom Outside the House

1. The guidelines above also apply to locations outside your home.
2. Talk about and roleplay how to manage peer pressure.

While implementing your agreements, expect some testing and manipulation. Expect a lot of testing if you have a fourteen-year-old son who is used to gaming six hours per day. On the other hand, praise cooperation and don't model ridiculous tech involvement yourself.

Technology: Managing Problems

If violations of your family agreement occur, consider one-on-one meetings first and then perhaps consider the Major/Minor System for repeat offenses. As it is with the other three big risks, though, trying to control your kids' tech involvement is fraught with problems. Adolescents can easily use a friend's computer or mobile device to access sites you don't want them to access. They can use your mobile devices as well, and they can Google "circumvent parental controls" for up-to-date advice and chat on how to do just that.

Just like your teenagers, however, you too can access free and helpful experts. They're called other parents. All you have to do is make a few phone calls. School counselors or pediatricians may also help hook you up with someone. Here's what you'll find. About half of the parents you talk to won't be any help because they won't know any more than you do. Twenty-five percent will be somewhat useful, and the final twenty-five percent or so will be very useful! What question do you ask them? This one: "How do you handle all this new tech stuff with your kids and what do you do about parental controls?" After reading this chapter, using another sympathetic and friendly human being as a guide is the most efficient—and easiest!—way to attack the issue of teens and tech.

In managing problems regarding technology, though, you should have one primary concern: Your ability to maintain an open and friendly relationship with the kids is critical. A protracted parent-teen war over tech can become a lot like spying and espionage. You might even find it kind of fun at times! The problem? You are almost certain not only to lose the war but also to lose your relationship with your adolescent in the process. That will hurt both of you.

So there you have it: Driving, drugs and alcohol, sex and romance and constantly changing technology. You want to prevent as many problems as you reasonably can but also be able to manage issues that do come up. And you have to do this with a kid who a lot of the time doesn't seem to want to have much to do with you. Remember that risk and rejection are naturally irritating to all parents. Risk and rejection are also a normal part of adolescence. Before you try to manage any scary problems, you have to first learn to manage your own thoughts and feelings.

CHAPTER 11

Your Teens Have Their MBAs!

Not all problems are created equal. After discussing House Rules and things like the Big Four Risks, it may be a relief to go to the other end of the spectrum. We have good news for you: Your teens have their MBAs.

If you suspect a trick here, you are correct. Many things that adolescents do—or don't do—fall into the "MBA" category. That means they are "Minor But Aggravating." It's very important for parents to keep in mind that their level of aggravation about a problem is not always a measure of the seriousness of that problem. Just because you get ferociously angry about something, in other words, doesn't mean it is a sign of a major character flaw, mental illness or sociopathic tendencies in your offspring. It may be just an irritating part of normal adolescence.

What kinds of problems fall into the MBA category? One of the best examples is the use of the phone. Do you know that long, pointless and apparently stupid conversations between teenagers over the phone are normal and healthy? Endless dialogues are what kids are supposed to be doing at this age!

The cell phone rings and your sixteen-year-old daughter dives for it. The following conversation ensues:

"Hello."

"Hi. What are you doing?"

"Nothing. What are you doing?"

"Nothing."

"Cool."

Two hours later not much more of significance is being discussed, but everything's still cool. You, however, are not cool. You begin fuming, thinking about the phone bill and about how your daughter could better spend her time doing extra-credit work for biology.

Relax. Conversations like this are good for kids. They are making contact with each other. They are learning how to handle relationships. These connections are good for their self-esteem. Would you rather they weren't talking to anyone?

If you're concerned about the phone bill, make a deal that the kids pay for any charges over a certain amount per month. Otherwise, leave them alone or don't listen.

Another MBA-type "problem" has to do with dress and appearance. This issue involves clothing, hair, earrings and other attachments to or through the body and pants falling off. It's not reasonable to expect your teens to want to dress like you. Remember, often part of their thinking is that they want to look as different from you as possible.

QUIK TIP

It's not for us to define your list of MBAs. What's important is for you to understand the MBA concept first, and then to decide what items you will place on the list. There's a lot of potential relief in that little exercise!

One solution to the appearance problem: the kids can wear anything that the school will let them in the door with. Of course, schools' criteria are not too strict these days, but this policy does offer some control.

Another MBA? That messy room. What a pit! Your stomach writhes in agony every time you look at it. You have forgotten what color the carpet is. The cat was last seen in there three weeks ago. Do you know that there are no studies that prove that teens with messy rooms grow up to be homeless persons or schizophrenics or have a higher divorce rate than the rest of the population?

A possible solution? It may be to close the door and don't look. Or leave the door open and close your eyes as you go past. A sloppy bedroom is aggravating, but it isn't really a major problem. Also, be realistic. If all the nagging and arguing and lecturing you've done over the years hasn't convinced your seventeen-year-old son to clean his room regularly, he probably isn't going to start now no matter what you do. We respectfully suggest that you have lost the battle. It's not the end of the world, and you don't want arguing about a messy room to be the end of your relationship.

If you already have your own rules about the MBAs we have mentioned so far, and your rules are working just fine, pay no attention to the advice here. What does "working just fine" mean? Two things. First, the rules are not unreasonably restrictive. Second, the rules do not result in a lot of arguing.

Other Possible MBAs

Here are some other probable Minor-But-Aggravating issues that you might consider staying away from:

- Musical preferences
- Grammar
- Not going on family outings
- Intermittent negative attitude

- Eating habits
- Use of allowance
- Using your things
- Forgetfulness with chores

Certainly these problems can all be aggravating—in fact, very aggravating—but they should not necessarily be taken as indications that your child is emotionally disturbed. Remember this cardinal rule for parents of adolescents—especially as the kids get older: Never open your mouth unless you have a very good reason.

On the list of other possible MBAs are things like arguing, bedtime, swearing and bumming around town. These items may or may not be serious, depending on your situation. They are usually less serious the more competent your teenager is, the better your relationship with the child is, and the better you are doing yourself.

By the way, can you guess which two problems bug parents the most? Not drugs and drinking, and not smoking. In our surveys the "winners" are consistently arguing and sibling rivalry. This does not, of course, mean they are the most serious—simply the most frequently infuriating.

When you think about it, it's not really the place of a book like this to tell you what your list of MBAs should be. But our purpose is to acquaint you with the MBA concept, so you and your adolescent can get some relief from the idea as you see fit. Check "Managing Other Issues" in the Appendix for more thoughts

What Are Not MBAs

Adolescence is difficult enough for kids and their parents, but sometimes certain psychological problems—which are definitely not MBAs—are added to the picture. These can cause intense suffering for adolescents as well as their parents. Parents should not try to manage these difficulties on their own; professional evaluation and counseling are usually essential. **These more serious, non-MBA problems include the following:**

Anxiety Disorders: Some children are biologically predisposed to have excessive fears. These anxieties can relate to social situations, separation, obsessive thoughts and life in general.

Depression: True clinical depression involves a consistently gloomy view of life and, in adolescents, persistent irritability. It lowers self-esteem, takes the joy out of things, and is often accompanied by appetite and sleeping disturbances, social withdrawal and underachievement.

Attention Deficit Disorder: Definitely the most common childhood and adolescent problem. The poor concentration skills and frequent intense temperaments of these children can affect all areas of their lives—at school, at home, and with peers.

Conduct Disorder: A euphemism for what used to be called "juvenile delinquency." CD kids are defiant, abuse the rights of others and prematurely act out in areas such as sex, drugs, stealing and fighting. These children blame everyone else for their problems.

Eating Disorders: Anorexic girls refuse to maintain a normal body weight and have very distorted images of their own bodies, seeing fat where none exists. Bulimics can maintain a normal weight but often engage in binge-purge routines that jeopardize their physical health and trigger intense shame. Many girls—and a few guys—have characteristics of both anorexia and bulimia.

Alcohol and Drug Abuse: It is common for teens to experiment with alcohol and marijuana. Some, however, overuse these substances or use them in combination on a regular basis. A major problem exists when the drug use becomes a central life activity for the adolescent, especially when this use interferes with school, social, work and family life.

Divorce-Related Problems: Kids are resilient, but recent evidence suggests that parents' divorce can be especially traumatic for some children. When remarriages are involved, adolescents are harder to merge into the "blended family," sometimes causing extreme stress on second marriages.

Sexual Abuse: Estimates of the percentage of girls who have been sexually abused vary widely, but there is no doubt the number is high. The effects on a child can include precocious sexual activity, chronic guilt, poor interpersonal relationships and low self-esteem.

These kinds of issues are not MBAs. As you can see, one of the hard parts of being a parent is knowing when to keep quiet and when to get involved. If you're worried but just not sure, talk to a counselor—perhaps by yourself—and determine if you can relax or if something needs to be done.

SOLUTION: Chatty Cathy

Remember our six kids from Chapter 8? Well, we just solved our first case—the case of Chatty Cathy. Cathy's talking on the phone is an MBA. She's a good kid; leave her alone and enjoy her enthusiasm!

CHAPTER 12

Possible Intervention Roles

When something about your teenager is bothering you, stop and think before doing or saying anything. Shooting from the hip can cause a lot of trouble. You need to ask yourself three questions:

1. Does this problem need my attention or intervention?
2. If it does, how involved should I get?
3. Is the adolescent Snub affecting my feelings at all?

There are basically four caps a parent can wear when responding to a problem. These options vary in their level of intrusiveness. From least intrusive to most invasive they are:

- Observer
- Advisor
- Negotiator
- Director

Option 1: Observer

As an observer, you are really not intervening at all in your adolescent's life. You are trusting your child to handle things. Your daughter, for example, has a new friend that you don't particularly care for, but your daughter is generally a competent kid and you respect her opinion. Or your son is getting to bed somewhat later than he used to. You're worried that it may affect him during the day, but so far he seems OK. You can keep a watchful eye on what's happening. If worse comes to worse, you may proceed to an Advisor or Negotiator role. The Observer role, of course, is appropriate for MBAs.

Being in the observer role does not rule out sympathetic listening. Sympathetic listening is an excellent idea anyway for basically competent kids and nonessential problems, such as a diet, a friend you don't like, or a temporary drop in a grade. Phinicky Phils' mother, for example, knows here son is a responsible kid. She's going to be sympathetic and give a little bit of advice, but basically she's going to stay out and trust him to do what he thinks is best:

How great is that! No nagging, pushing, lectures about disrespect or threats of punishment. Instead, Phil gets sympathy and a complete vote of confidence. Is Phil more dangerous to anybody after this conversation? Definitely not. He's on his way to solving the problem himself.

When you want to simply observe but you're still troubled, you can help yourself let go by using what we call the "Awful Scale." Here you create a kind of subjective/objective scale that ranges from 0 to 100, and you use it to rate the "awfulness" of different events that might happen in your life. In other words, you are rating how miserable different things might make you. Something rated 0, for example, would not bother you at all. A rating of 15 would be a minor hassle, while a rating of 85 would indicate an extremely taxing situation. An event qualifying for a score of 100 would be something that would make you permanently miserable.

Once you have the general idea of the Awful Scale, you need to practice rating different incidents or circumstances. What would you rate a flat tire on your car at the end of a long work day? Some people say 10, some 20 or 30. What if you broke your right arm, and you are right handed? 30 or 40? What if your house burned down? Most folks say 60 or 70. What if your spouse died? Some people say, "It depends on the day," but most people put a loss like this in the 90 to 95 category.

Do you know what almost all parents consider to be the worst thing that could happen to them? The death of a child. People will say "That would be 130," or "I can't even imagine it." But most parents agree that it would be as close to 100 as anything can get.

With this perspective in mind we return to some of the actual problems that parents are concerned with in their children. Your son comes home sporting new blue hair and carrying a progress report with two Fs on it. What would you rate that? Many parents say something like, "Why that little creep! That's an 85 or 90 easy!" Using the Awful Scale, at this point I would try to point out that the rating for the hair and the grades is only 10 or 15 points away from the rating for the death of the child, which obviously can't make any sense! What is needed is another long look at how bad the problem really is. What usually happens is that—upon further review and with clearer thinking—the original rating has to be dropped considerably.

Option 2: Advisor (Consultant)

In the world of business a consultant is a person who is hired to give advice. There are two conditions to the contract. First, the consultant will be paid for his work. Second, the person who receives the advice has the right to accept or reject it. Except for the pay, consultant is the role we are talking about in this chapter for parents of adolescents.

"I wish you'd cut your hair shorter," "Please clean your room this weekend," "If you want my opinion, I think you're trying to push your boyfriend around too much," and "I think it would be a good idea if you got your homework done before we leave" are all potentially legitimate consultant statements. They are attempts to give advice, and with fairly good relationships, the parent/consultant stands a good chance of at least being heard. As an advisor, however, you are still only a consultant to the child, which means you are not using power and the adolescent has the right to reject your advice.

If your advice or request doesn't change the situation, you have two alternatives (neither alternative is to repeat your "advice" over and over). With small problems, you may just go back to being an observer and perhaps the "Grin and Bear It" approach. If, on the other hand, you feel the issue is more important, you may want to go on to the next parent role, that of negotiator.

If you are going to consider trying to be an advisor to your child, don't shoot from the hip. There are a few considerations you should think over before you open your mouth. You recall in an earlier scene Mary's mother didn't care for the way her boyfriend was treating her daughter. But the Mom sprung her advice unexpectedly on Mary, which resulted in a bitter argument.

Let's watch Mom do the Advisor role correctly:

Mary is not thrilled at all with Mom's comments, but at least she heard them. And no inflammatory argument followed to make Mary more enraged and vulnerable. She's still in charge of her relationship with her boyfriend.

If you think consulting is the appropriate role for you with this child and this problem, clarify out loud before any discussion that you only want to talk, that you may or may not give any advice, and that any advice you may give can be used or not—as your youngster sees fit. Make up your mind that you will only be a consultant. This commitment will help you not feel like a wimpy parent, and it will also help you to not mistakenly jump into a heavier role—like Director—if the teenager makes you angry. Clarifying your role will also make your adolescent less defensive, since she will be assured that the final decision will be hers.

In any discussion about a problem, if the teen agrees to talk, you want to always listen to him first. Unfortunately, it may be true that few teens are going to want to listen to your opinions much to begin with. You increase your chances of being listened to, however, by having the patience to hear your children out before you speak.

Option 3: Negotiator

The beginning of an attempt at negotiation might go something like this: "We've got a problem here and I'd like to talk it over with you sometime." What you are doing here is recognizing that the child is older now and that he should have more say about many of the things that he does. Negotiating is also a statement that you feel it is important to be involved, because you think the problem is serious (it's not an MBA!) or it affects other family members. But you are saying that—up to a point—you are willing to bargain or make a deal.

Although negotiating doesn't have to be anything horribly fancy, it is critical that you follow certain minimal guidelines. Remember the rule outlawing attempts at spontaneous problem-solving discussions, and never insist on an immediate talk unless a total emergency exists. Also, don't bring up the idea of having a talk when you are already pretty cranked out of shape about something. Chances are your teen will go nuclear on you, and it will be just that much harder to bring the issue up again.

How do you broach the subject of making a deal with the kids? Imagine these possibilities:

"When's a good time for you to talk with me about the leftover food in your room? It's starting to smell up there."

"You may not be too thrilled by this suggestion, but sometime in the next couple of days I want to sit down with you and talk about college."

"I can't say I care for your new work schedule too much. Can we go over it together sometime?"

"We gotta talk about your smoking. Not now, but tell me when's good."

In responding to these opening comments, kids may attempt to talk about the problem prematurely. When they are caught off guard like this, however, it is unlikely that you are going to have a profitable pow-wow. It is more likely that—in the interests of their budding independence—the youngsters are simply going to try to get you off their backs as quickly as possible. They can do this in two ways. The first is to try to minimize your worries and make light of the problem:

"What's the big deal?"

"Oh, Mom."

"Just chill out, will ya? I'll take care of it."

"Now, don't start bugging me about that again."

You, however, have already thought it over and have decided the problem is important or you wouldn't have brought it up, right? So you respond to these comments by telling the teen that you don't want to discuss the issue right away but that you do feel that it is important. When is a good time for her? Don't get suckered into talking about the problem with an uncooperative adolescent.

The second way the teen may try to get rid of you is to attempt to provoke a fight:

"Why don't you just mind your own affairs instead of running the whole world? You shouldn't be in my room in the first place!"

"Did I pick where you went to college? Just butt out."

"Why are you always ragging at me? I don't see where my work schedule is any of your business. Do I tell you when to show up at that dump you work at?"

"You smoked when you were a kid. Better be careful—you're the one living in the glass house, lady!"

When confronted with responses like these, don't get sidetracked and stumble dumbly into one or more of the Four Cardinal Sins. *You are being baited.* Keep in mind what your major goal is here (it's not murder). Your objective is only to make an appointment with the youngster to talk. If she refuses to talk, and you still feel the problem is important, you will be going on to the Director role.

Once you've agreed to talk, pick a good time and place. Go to a quiet room, take the adolescent out somewhere, or even go to dinner. Often a long ride in the car is an excellent idea (you don't have to look directly at each other), and make sure you let the teen drive if they can. It's great if you can plan something enjoyable to do after the discussion, but this idea doesn't always work. Make sure there won't be interruptions from other family members or any possibility of phone calls.

Puffing Penny's mother decides on the car-ride-plus-food idea:

Daughter's driving—good start. Mom defines the problem, then listens first. She doesn't go rattling on and getting all excited. If you keep trying to talk to your kids like that you'll never get anywhere with anything! How many times have I already said that you can't act that way!! Lectures don't work!!! I don't know what it's going to take for you as a parent to get it through your head that this kind of thing...

Oops. The Four Cardinal Sins are very seductive. Where were we? The teen is talking first and you are listening. Give her five to ten minutes, longer usually isn't necessary. Don't interrupt, roll your eyes or make faces like she's an idiot. Simply listening and not arguing does not have to imply that you agree with everything the adolescent is saying. Be sure to ask good, nonjudgmental questions.

You may not like what you hear. Try to keep your cool, but if you find yourself really upset after the teen has talked, say something like, "Listen, a lot of what you said is new to me and I need some time to think it over. Give me a day to get used to all this, and then maybe we can sit down and we'll try to finish it."

If you're not too upset, ask the child not to interrupt you while you take five or ten minutes to explain your side of things. Stay calm and try not to accuse or blame.

Assuming you've gotten through the earlier negotiation phases alive and with the problem clarified, you must now come up with a solution. Sometimes, if you're lucky, you may not need a solution because you learned that the thing was not as big a deal as you thought. But usually you won't be this fortunate.

To bargain or make a deal, don't get too pushy about your own ideas—even if you feel they're just brilliant. Try to get the teen to make suggestions first and give these ideas careful consideration. You

might start the solution-oriented part of the negotiation by saying something like:

"Well, it's obvious we don't agree, but that doesn't mean we can't come up with some compromise. What do you think?"

"Tell me what you think would be fair to you and everybody else."

"What kind of arrangement do you think would work here?"

The sign of a good bargain is that there is something in it for everyone, but everyone has to give up a little something, too. The best solution is one that the teen devises that also helps you feel better. If you can't agree with your child's initial proposal, support the good parts of his idea and suggest some modifications.

Here are some examples of possible bargains:

1. **Loud music.** Dad agrees to buy Mark headphones for the stereo if Mark will promise to wear them—and not use his large speakers—whenever anyone else is home.

2. **Phone.** Melissa can talk on the phone as much as she wants as long as her grades don't drop below a 2.50 GPA and as long as she pays any extra amount over $50 a month on phone bills.

3. **Smoking.** Mom and Dad agree to stop nagging eighteen-year-old Tom about his smoking, as long as he no longer smokes in the house.

4. **Hair.** Parents will pay for Jim's haircut as long as the mop is not left more than two inches below his collar.

What if the teen doesn't want to suggest anything, becomes belligerent or feels there's no problem? You have a choice. You can go back to the Observer role (forget giving more advice). You can grin and bear it using the Awful Scale, cultivating and refining your toleration of nonessential differences. Or you can move on to taking charge (the Director role).

If you are able to come up with a solution, it's helpful to write it down. Some people even sign it like a contract. Though the kids often feel this technique is stupid, try to write out the agreement anyway. This small exercise helps you remember what you said (it's not always easy) and it makes the agreement feel more solid.

If your agreement works well, some brief, friendly positive reinforcement from time to time will be in order. For example:

"I think our little deal is working well so far."

"You're keeping your part of our bargain about college so far. Do you think your Dad and I are?"

"You seem OK with the new work schedule. Is that true?"

"I don't know about you, but I think—after three weeks of no arguments—that we may have solved that smoking problem."

If the deal doesn't work, don't have a fit. Go back to the drawing board, keep the good parts of your arrangement, and see if you can agree on the necessary changes. Follow the negotiation format described above. And while you're doing all this, continue to not take The Snub personally.

Option 4: Director

There may be times when you feel an issue with a teen is very serious and the adolescent is not able to handle the problem. Perhaps attempts to talk things over have not worked out. Under these circumstances you may have to turn to the Director role. Because of teenagers' fierce desire to run their own lives, give this role a lot of thought before attempting to intervene.

The Director role can take three forms. Sometimes it may involve the Major/Minor System, which we discussed in Chapter 9. The other two forms are professional evaluation/counseling and not living together.

Professional Evaluation and Counseling

In Chapter 11 we considered that problems such as ADHD, depression, Conduct Disorder and drug abuse are certainly not MBAs. Parents of adolescents who have these difficulties will benefit from professional guidance and direction. Other emotional and behavioral problems teens can experience result from psychosis (such as schizophrenia), sexual or gender problems, physical abuse and bipolar illness. These issues can be heartbreaking and they are nothing to trifle with. A good rule of thumb is: If you as a parent have been persistently worried for longer than six months about the possibility of a psychological problem in your son or daughter, you have waited too long. Find someone you trust and get an opinion.

Unfortunately, counselors vary a lot in their approaches and personalities, so you may need to shop around. Getting an initial referral from a friend, doctor or local mental health center may be a good way to start. Don't use the yellow pages first unless you have no other recourse. Call several counselors, briefly describe the situation, and see how you like these folks over the phone. If these people can't give you a few minutes on the phone, forget them.

When discussing the possibility of counseling with an adolescent, never say to the teen, "You need help" or "We're going to get you some help." The word "help" is a sure way to turn anyone off! After all, no teen wants to see a shrink in the first place. Instead, you have a couple of other choices for bringing up this touchy subject, depending on what kind of relationship you have with the teen.

If your relationship isn't so hot, you might say "We're obviously doing a lousy job around here of working out our problems ourselves, so I think we'll see a professional of some sort and get their opinion about what to do." Don't argue about it, just set up the appointment.

If you are primarily concerned about your teenager—whatever your relationship is like—you had best be honest. "I'm worried about how you're feeling. Lately you don't seem to be yourself at all—too down, no fun, sleeping too much and much more irritable. I'm going to ask you to talk to somebody, and probably your Mom and I will too."

This is what Crabby Carl's parents did:

Sooner or later, most kids will go to visit a therapist. If the child refuses, you might want to go yourself first and ask the counselor what to do, though it is preferable with teenagers for the child to be seen before the parents. If the teen continues to refuse, you might use the Major/Minor System. For example, "You won't use the car again until you see the counselor at least for the evaluation."

One doctor who often referred people to other professionals suggested a good rule of thumb for selecting a counselor: remember that you are the consumer with the power of choice, and if you have seen someone three times and still don't like him or her, go find someone else.

Hospitalization may need to be considered if the problem is serious enough, and especially if you worry about your child hurting herself. Suicidal threats should always be taken seriously. The rate of teen suicide has increased in recent decades; the most vulnerable adolescents tend to be behaviorally-disturbed males who also abuse alcohol and drugs, depressed females, ambitious but socially isolated perfectionists, and kids who are bullied. The risk is always greater where there is a family history of suicide and/or a previous suicidal attempt or gesture by the child. Danger signs for suicide include the following:

- suicidal threats
- recent loss: family member, pet, boyfriend or girlfriend
- a sense of hopelessness
- loss of interest and/or energy
- preoccupation with death
- social withdrawal
- family disruption: divorce, illness, geographical moves
- giving away valuable possessions

Unfortunately, suicide has become a significant cause of death among teens. These suicides are not usually impulsive; before any self-destructive action is carried out, the teen has usually given it a lot of thought.

Kick Them Out

Most of us parents have a kind of rule in our heads that says family members are supposed to like one another, get along and stay together—at least until the kids are grown. Unfortunately, it doesn't always work out like that. Sometimes a teenager is simply too unruly and uncooperative. Sometimes parent/teen chemistry, for whatever reason, is simply rotten, even though both people seem to be doing well separately.

If and when it comes time to seriously consider not living with their adolescent anymore, moms and dads always feel an acute sense of failure. But as they say in the "Tough Love" programs, parents are people, too, and we all have limited emotional resources. There's no benefit in blaming yourself for everything that went wrong in the past. The kids, after all, never were really putty in your hands. If everything didn't turn out the way you wanted it to, there were certainly many different reasons.

Unless the child himself chooses to leave (at an appropriate age, of course), there are a few alternatives for parents who have concluded they shouldn't live with their teenager anymore. These options involve parents in the Director role, and they are not easy to enact.

> **CAUTION** ⚠️
> You don't kick a teen out of the house on the spur of the moment during a fight or argument, unless there has been physical violence. The procedure takes more thought and planning than that.

Where bad parent/teen chemistry is the main issue and the adolescent in question still gets along well with other adults, some families have tried to negotiate living arrangements with other relatives or with friends. Maybe old Uncle Joe in Michigan's Upper Peninsula needs a little company. Negotiating should be used here as well as it can be with the adolescent and the other family, so that house rules, money and other living arrangements are perfectly clear before the move.

When living at home is intolerable, though, moving in with another family is not usually a realistic alternative. A second possibility is a boarding school, military school or other treatment facility where kids can stay. Two big problems here are finding a good one and paying for it. Contact a school or local mental health center to locate some possibilities and be sure to visit any place before considering it.

A final alternative applies to late (age eighteen and older) adolescents only: Kick the teen out of the house. This advice may sound terrible, and booting a child out is more emotionally difficult for everyone than residential placement, but under really trying circumstances, taking this important step may actually be in the best interests of both parents and adolescent. By this time the "child" is really an adult, and he will have to be responsible—come hell or high water—for his own problems.

How do you kick a person out of his own house? You don't do it on the spur of the moment during a fight or argument, unless, perhaps, there has been physical violence. What is sometimes done is a version of the Major/Minor System, where the ultimate consequence of poor behavior is having to leave home for good. You will need some help from both an attorney and from a mental health professional. The attorney is for the legal part of the process and the mental health professional is for the guilt.

You recall Obnoxious Arnie? His parents had finally had enough. So they wrote a note (or sometimes a lawyer writes the first note) saying something like this:

If the young person can stick to the rules, fine. The odds, however, are 99 percent that Arnie won't be able to—or even want to—do this. So when the inevitable Major infraction occurs, they will be prepared, with their attorney's help, to give their son notice. Some "kids" will get mad at a letter like the one above, tear it up and screw up right away. They are then given notice.

What if the difficult son or daughter won't leave? You get an attorney who writes a letter to your young adult informing him that he is of age and has been asked to leave, and that refusing to do so will be regarded as trespassing. It's no fun—in fact, it's horrible for Mom and Dad—but it works. It's your house, after all, and you have a right to protect your belongings, the other children at home for whom you are responsible, and yourselves. What if the "kid" won't leave by the time stated in the letter? Your attorney can instruct you about how the courts and the police can remove *anyone* who is illegally in your house.

In this chapter we've solved four more of our sample cases:

SOLUTION: Phinicky Phil

Phil's a good kid and a competent kid. He doesn't really need a big parental intervention. Mom will remain largely in an **Observer** capacity after taking one brief shot at the **Advisor** role. Mostly she's going to support her son in making his own decision.

SOLUTION: Puffing Penny

Penny's mother's first good move is not to nag or lecture. Then she's going to use the **Negotiator** role and she will listen respectfully to her daughter's opinion first. But Penny's not going to smoke in the house. Mom will be ready to firmly employ the Major/Minor System (**Director** role) if negotiation fails.

SOLUTION: Crabby Carl

Carl looks like he might be depressed following the breakup with his girlfriend. His parents do well not to return his crabbiness in kind (sort of like avoiding the Snub-Resnub routine). But they are ready to take the **Director** role and make sure that their son sees a counselor quickly.

SOLUTION: Obnoxious Arnie

Arnie is too much for anybody to take! With the help of an attorney and a mental health professional, his parents are going to calmly develop a strategy for dealing with their own guilt while they systematically confront their son and get him out of the house.

PART IV

Stay in Touch

CHAPTER 13

What *Not To* Do: The Four Cardinal Sins

We saw before that the twin issues of rejection and risk tend to regularly irritate parents. If Mom and Dad don't work hard to think straight about these matters, their irritation can produce lots of bad outcomes. Among them are what we call "The Four Cardinal Sins."

Mark and his son, seventeen-year-old John, used to be fairly close until John hit fourteen or so. Now things are different: friends are primary, parents an afterthought. It's a school day evening and John is heading toward the front door with his coat. Mark thinks: "What can he possibly want to do at this time of night? No time for his old man anymore." Right away he's annoyed. The following scene occurs at the front door:

"Where are you going?"

"Out with the guys."

"What guys? You know it's already 8:30."

"I know."

"Who you going with?"

"Tom, Dick and Harry."

"I'm serious, pal."

"Mike and maybe Bobby."

"Maybe Bobby? Oh, really?! Why does that idiot always have to go along? How many times have I told you that kid's trouble, but you don't ever want to listen to me, do you? Where are you guys going?"

"McDonald's."

"What do you need at McDonald's? We just finished eating dinner."

"We're just going to hang out."

"Wonderful. That's how half the trouble starts in this town. Kids bumming around with nothing to do. I assume your homework's done."

"Perfectly, precisely and brilliantly."

"Listen, wise guy, I just asked a simple question."

"I'm outta here."

"You get your majesty back at a decent hour — you hear me? Or there'll be plenty of trouble around here!"

Ouch!

In the conversation we just heard, Dad is not aware of his own irritation toward his son and the reasons for it (rejection and risk). So the annoyed parent becomes overly conscientious, self-righteous and basically silly. In the process Dad commits all four of the Cardinal Sins:

1. Spur-of-the-Moment Problem Discussions

2. Nagging

3. Insight Transplants

4. Arguing

The Four Cardinal Sins are primitive and impulsive emotional responses that occur without much thought. The Four Cardinal Sins don't accomplish anything, except to place an adolescent more at risk by irritating the daylights out of him. Mark's poorly-thought-out questions and comments actually *increased*—rather than *decreased*—the chances of John's getting hurt himself or his hurting someone else.

What should Dad have done at the front door? He should have first thought, "I'm not going to take this personally. He's supposed to be more focused on friends at his age. I was when I was a teen." Next, if issues such as homework or hours are not clear, they should be discussed and clarified *at some other time*. Finally, the only thing Mark should have said was, "See you later. Have a good time!"

If, as a midlife parent, you yourself are doing poorly and are under too much stress, you may very well be committing the Four Cardinal Sins on a regular basis. Your behavior will make life worse for everybody, including you. Let's take a closer look at each of these blunders.

Spur-of-the-Moment Problem Discussions

When you become aware of a problem with an adolescent, you simply mention it to the kid, right? Wrong! Here's a common scene—progress report time:

"How ya doin'?"

"Fine?"

"So, what's this about an F in biology? I just got your progress report in the mail."

"It's no big deal. Must be some kind of mistake."

"I don't think so. Remember we went through this last semester."

"No I don't remember, frankly. All I know is I came in here to get a sandwich and you jump on me!"

"I'm not jumping on you at all. So don't start giving me that, young lady! If I didn't take the responsibility sometimes for your schoolwork!!!"

Here the well-meaning parent sees a problem and, naturally, says something about it. What the parent is saying is perfectly valid and not intended to cause trouble.

The catch? The odds that the adolescent is also motivated to discuss this unpleasant subject at this time are zero. In fact, spontaneous problem discussions almost always increase irritability and decrease cooperation. The child is usually doing something else—even if it's only watching TV—and it takes a while to get "psyched" for talking about something unpleasant. It is a fact of human nature. Chances are you feel the same way about people interrupting you with unpleasant things. What would you expect the girl to say, "Gee, thanks for reminding me about that darn old F in bio. Your concern for my academic welfare is heartwarming"?

Sometimes spontaneous talks are unavoidable, but in general you need to make an appointment with your adolescent to discuss an important problem. Tell her—short and sweet—what you want to talk about, and agree on a time to get together. Take her out to eat if you want. This is a better approach:

> *"I'm concerned about your grade in biology. When would be a good time to talk this over?"*

Nagging

The second of our Cardinal Sins is nagging. Nagging can be defined as a set of repetitive, often hostile verbal reminders about something that a parent wants to see accomplished. Nagging is often directed at a teenager who does not share the parent's enthusiasm for the project. And, as is the case with the first Cardinal Sin, nagging usually occurs on the spur of the moment:

> *"Is this a bedroom or a pigsty?"*
>
> *"Come on."*
>
> *"How many times have I asked you!? What color is this carpet? You don't even know, do you?"*
>
> *"What's the big..."*
>
> *"You want to live like a slob all your life? Lemme tell you something: No woman is going to put up with the likes of you."*
>
> *"I'm trying to study..."*
>
> *"When you gonna learn you can't live like a pig? Don't you care about anything anymore? It gets worse and worse!"*

Behind nagging is a kind of psychotic parental delusion—the notion that repetition will make an idea or request sink in. If asking the teen twenty-two times to clean his room didn't work, maybe the twenty-third time will be the charm!

What is the antidote to nagging? First, don't open your mouth unless it's absolutely essential. Next, be sure that what you want to talk about is important (i.e., not an MBA). Then make an appointment.

Lectures (Insight Transplants)

The third Cardinal Sin often takes the form of a parental lecture. In the scene below, Obnoxious Arnie's father gets a hold of his offspring and explains the facts of life to him:

"When are you gonna get a job?"

"I don't know."

"You know you're going to be twenty your next birthday. That's a two followed by a little zero. You understand what I'm saying?"

"Yeah, yeah, yeah."

"Listen, when I was your age, we had to work. Had to. No choice. Everybody contributed. Everybody pitched in to get the job done. What about you? You sit around here. You ain't got a job. You don't go to school. No, you make sex phone calls all night and have the bill sent to me. That's just great, that's just great!"

"Why don't you just shut up!!"

"You know, if you had a place to go, I'd throw your fat butt outta this house!"

What Dad is thinking—or hoping—goes something like this: "I will take this wonderful insight I have learned regarding life, put it into words, and send it through the air waves. It will enter my child's ears and proceed to his brain where it will take root, flower and subsequently generate new and more productive behavior."

That would certainly be nice, but it's not going to happen. The point is not that what the parent is saying is stupid. On the contrary, Dad's main point here is sensible. But saying it (especially as he did) accomplishes nothing and causes trouble. Dad needs another plan of action.

I often suggest to parents who are inclined to lecture their children that they open their eyes and closely examine the face of their teen during the one-sided talk. Is there a scowl or a snicker there? Are the eyes rolling or is it the Great Stone Face? Many kids, instead of listening intently, are simply thinking, "Here's another repeat of item #43 from Father's Famous Lecture Series. How can I either shut him up or get out of here ASAP?"

What's the alternative to lecturing? For many situations, the best option is to make sure the issue is important and then make an appointment to discuss it. Obnoxious Arnie's circumstances, though, are different. His parents are going to kick him out of the house.

Arguing

A psychologist friend of mine once said that the best advice he could give to parents of adolescents was to never argue with their teens. This is probably an excellent suggestion. The three other Cardinal Sins often give birth to major arguments, which damage relationships further and sometimes even lead to physical encounters. Surveys of parents asking what is the most aggravating problem with their adolescents often reveal that arguing is #1.

In the scene below, Mom really, really doesn't like her daughter's boyfriend. He makes her skin crawl and Mom feels her daughter is being abused. So it's off to the races:

"Mary, you know I've been thinking about you and Bob."

"Yeah?"

"When are you going to break up with him?"

"What do you mean?"

"You know what I mean. He's kind of a jerk, don't you think?"

"Mom, it's not really any of your business."

"Oh, yes it is my business when my own daughter's being treated like dirt!"

"He's not that bad, Mom, and you know it!"

"No I don't know it. He's just using you. When are you going to wake up?!"

"And what would you know, you never had a boyfriend in high school anyway."

"I had my chances. Besides, I had some taste."

"Well, thanks a lot!"

Parents often ask, "If we're not supposed to argue, what are we supposed to do? Just keep our mouths shut and let the kids have their way?" Definitely not. When it is essential, you must try to see to it that your children are doing what they are supposed to, but it's very rare for anyone to be argued into submission. Arguing usually results in battle lines being firmly drawn. Each person's ideas become more and more extreme, and sometimes the combatants start saying things they don't even mean. The whole point of the "discussion" becomes to win and, if possible, to find some clever way of making your opponent look stupid.

What are your alternatives? We'll discuss more options soon. But to begin with, don't start a conversation that is bound to go nowhere, as our frustrated mother just did. She knows how her daughter feels about her advice.

If you surveyed teenagers, you'd probably find that The Four Cardinal Sins top their list of obnoxious parental behaviors. The real issue here, though, is that while the Four Cardinal Sins don't solve anything, they do ruin relationships and, most importantly, *they compromise your kids' safety by increasing the adolescent's desire to act up.* Surprisingly, these four blunders can also be addictive, and if you do not eliminate them from your playbook, nothing much else in this book will do any good.

THE BASIC STRATEGY FOR DEALING WITH THE FOUR CARDINAL SINS IS THE FOLLOWING:

1. IF THE PROBLEM YOU WANT TO DISCUSS IS AN MBA, KEEP QUIET.

2. IF THE ISSUE IS IMPORTANT, MAKE AN APPOINTMENT.

3. IF THE DISCUSSION BECOMES AN ARGUMENT, SAY "THIS CONVERSATION IS SILLY, I'M HISTORY," AND LEAVE.

CHAPTER 14

What *To* Do

You're concerned about your teen's safety and, naturally, you would like to get along with him as well as possible. By this time, however, you realize that he is determined to pull away from you and live his own life. You know there are limits on how close you can be during these years. But you are no longer taking the increased distance and The Snub personally, and you have resolved not to make the hostility/distance wall any bigger by engaging in the Four Cardinal Sins.

So what *can* you do to try to maintain a reasonably open and friendly relationship? Though none of these "tactics" is particularly easy (especially with someone who is avoiding you!), here are four positive substitutes for the Four Cardinal Sins:

           1. Sympathetic Listening

           2. Talking About Yourself

           3. Shared Fun

           4. Positive Reinforcement

In healthy relationships, these kinds of interactions probably happen more or less automatically and regularly. If your relationship with your child needs some work, however, and if you think you have the time and energy, give these ideas some thought.

Sympathetic Listening

Wouldn't you love to know what your teens are really thinking? Then again, maybe you wouldn't! Sympathetic—or active—listening is a way of talking to someone in which you try to accomplish two things: 1) an understanding of what another person is saying and thinking—even if you don't agree; and 2) a continual checking with the person you're listening to to make sure you are getting her message right. The listener is an active participant in the conversation rather than some shrink-like being who just sits and nods from time to time.

Good listening is not easy. But once you get past the point of feeling weird or artificial, you can sometimes pleasantly knock the kids right off their feet. Active listening should always be used at the beginning of any problem-solving discussion. People who do counseling or psychotherapy, for example, have to use active listening when meeting a client for the first time. If they don't, they won't get the critical information they need to help solve problems.

The same thing is true in dealing with a child: If you don't listen, you may not get important information you need to know in order to realistically attack a problem. But effective listening is a good thing in itself—people really appreciate being listened to and understood. Most of the time with your kids, your advice isn't needed.

Adolescents can sometimes say things that catch you off-guard. Some of these impromptu comments may be important and worth discussing. But if you're used to being snubbed and you're not expecting adolescent self-revelation in the first place, you can miss a good opportunity to talk. Here are three examples:

1) *"My soccer coach is such a jerk!"*
   "So what are you, a star athlete?"

2) *"This family is so boring."*
   "Well, you're not so hot yourself sometimes!"

3) *"You know, I don't think sex before marriage is so bad."*
   "Oh, that's just a great attitude!"

These parents won't get far in these conversations, and they honestly don't seem like they want to. The teens are turned off and The Snub will intensify. When you listen, on the other hand, you try to understand what the kids are saying and also let them know you understand. To accomplish the first goal of understanding, you can use what are called "openers" and you also use nonjudgmental questions. An opener can be an interested question, or it can simply be a comment like "Oh?" or "Really?" Let's redo the three scenes we just witnessed:

1) *"My soccer coach is such a jerk!"*
   "Why? What happened?"

2) *"This family is so boring."*
   "How long have you felt that way? What's going on?"

3) *"You know, I don't think sex before marriage is so bad."*
   "Oh yeah? I think you and I need a little pow-wow. Tell me what you're thinking."

These comments require self-control and are especially difficult when you are caught off-guard. They may also appear passive or wimpy to you, but remember that listening must precede any problem-solving discussion. If discipline or other action is necessary, worry about it after you've gotten the facts. But discipline and your advice are usually not needed.

Once the conversation has been opened, further nonjudgmental, sympathetic questions can keep it going. Here are some bad, judgmental questions:

1) Soccer coach: *"So what's your problem today?"*

2) Boring family: *"Why do you always hit me with the same old garbage?"*

3) Sex before marriage: *"Why are you obsessed with sex at your age?"*

These questions will inspire argument or silence. Here are some better questions that might keep the talk going:

1) Soccer coach: *"Is Coach Alex always like this?"*

2) Boring family: *"Why do you think we never do anything you like?"*

3) Sex before marriage: *"How many of your friends have had sexual relationships?"*

In print alone, of course, we can't describe the tone of voice that should accompany these questions, but it should be readily apparent that any of the above could be totally ruined by a sarcastic, angry, belittling or condescending tone of voice. It helps a lot to stay focused on your goal: Whether or not I agree, *what are they thinking?*

If you are making progress in understanding a teen's thoughts and feelings about something, your next goal is to check out your observations with the youngster. What are called summaries or perception checks can let her know that you can imagine how she must have felt under the circumstances she's describing. You may be accused of sounding like a shrink at times, but if you are, just say, "Sorry, but I'm just trying to make sure I understand what you're talking about," or, "Give me a break. I'm doing my best to figure out what you're saying!"

Imagine the three conversations above continuing. At some point in the discussion, the parent might have an opportunity to say:

1) *"You're not sure if you want to finish the soccer season."*

2) *"Sounds like you feel our family is almost depressing."*

3) *"You were really embarrassed thinking everyone else knew more about sex than you did."*

What you're doing here is sort of summarizing what's been said and then checking back with the adolescent to see if you're reading her right. Here are some other examples of checks or summaries:

1) *"What you're saying is that if Dad and I can smoke—and we know it's not good for us—you should be able to as well?"*

2) *"Sounds like you think you'll fit in more, and also perhaps look better, if you can get your nose pierced?"*

3) *"You think I don't really care much about my health anymore, and the main reason is what my job has done to me?"*

So from time to time during a talk, it is often helpful to test out with the teenager whether or not you are "catching her drift" or really getting a good idea of what she's saying. These kinds of comments let you know whether or not you're understanding her correctly, but they also have a second purpose: they tell the adolescent that you're really listening.

Sympathetic listening is a skill, but it's also an attitude: your attitude, not your child's. It's the attitude of sincerely trying to figure out what someone else is thinking even if you don't agree, or even if it drives you nuts. You're a good listener if you do that. You're a bad listener if, while the kid is talking, you are preparing your rebuttal.

Listen well and you might learn something new. Your teen will appreciate it and you'll also lower the hostility/distance wall a bit.

Oh, by the way. The question, "How was your day?" is still a bad question!

Talking About Yourself

With all this talk about parents' listening, it's easy to focus too much on your teenager. You can wind up feeling like you're trying to constantly "diagnose" the boy or girl to see if anything's going wrong. Teens quickly pick up on an overly solici- tous or overly inquisitive  attitude, and then they get defensive and The Snub gets worse.

One father described his son's behavior as "cave-itis," meaning that the boy spent almost all his time at home in his room. The cause for this withdrawal, it turned out, was that the boy didn't feel it was safe to come out! Every time he showed up, he was "greeted" with statements like, "Is your homework done?" "Where did you get that shirt?" "I think it's about time for a haircut" and "Can you give me a little help around here today?"

A good antidote to this kind of communication is to spontaneously talk about yourself. Horror of horrors! It's amazing how many parents seem to be almost phobic about discussing their own thoughts, concerns or problems with their children. This reticence is a shame, because many children of all ages would be very interested in hearing what their parents think about their jobs, their friends, about middle age or about something interesting that happened to them that day.

Just so you don't get overly self-conscious, pay attention to two things before you plunge into self-revelation. First, there can be no hidden message or moral in your story. Perhaps you were hoping that we had just come up with a sneaky way of getting some valuable point across. Sorry. That would only be a subtle version of one of the Four Cardinal Sins—the Insight Transplant routine. The point of your story can only be the inherent interest in the story itself.

Second, pick something interesting. If you just relax and let yourself be spontaneous, it may not be too hard to come up with something.

Your topic should be what you'd normally like to talk about anyway. How about:

"You won't believe what my boss said to me today!"

"Do you know I always hated biology?"

"I almost got into a fight in the Jewel parking lot this afternoon."

"When I was a kid, I used to love collecting baseball cards."

"I can't say I'm looking forward to my fortieth birthday."

"When I was your age, I sometimes worried that absolutely no one of the opposite sex was going to like me."

Some parents have trouble with opening up because they feel they don't want to burden their children with their problems, or they feel that—as parents—they are only supposed to be interested in their children. They may also have some kind of distorted idea that their children shouldn't know that Mom or Dad might be unhappy about something. This is the old "Keep a Stiff Upper Lip" notion of what a role model should be.

The Stiff Upper Lip is almost the same as trying to present yourself as perfect, above it all and able to handle anything. Can you see a problem with a parent coming across this way all the time, and combining that stance with a constant focus on the teen's problems? This kind of "I'm just fine, but you still need a lot of work" idea is great for creating belligerence in youngsters.

Some parents have trouble treating their kids as equals from time to time, even though such treatment might occasionally be appropriate. Consider the possibility that sometimes your kids might be able to sympathetically listen to you. Adolescents might even have some good advice, now and then, for Mom or Dad.

Should you tell your kids about the risk-taking behavior you engaged in as a teen? This is a tough question, but here's some advice. By all means don't present yourself to your kids as a former Straight Arrow if you really weren't one. Let the kids in on some of your secrets. That doesn't mean, of course, that you have to tell them every single stunt you pulled. On the other hand, if you have a rotten relationship with your teenage son or daughter, don't tell them anything. They'll simply use it against you or use it to justify their own acting out.

Shared Fun

Find any two people who regularly have fun together and you will find a good relationship. But finding a common activity both you and your teen can enjoy might be harder than finding one for you and your spouse! However, doing something together that you both enjoy is—to a relationship—like water and fertilizer to a plant. This notion may sound corny, but it makes perfect sense. For those having trouble find-ing something to do with a son or daughter, at the end of the chapter we'll tell you what activity is usually the simplest and best bet.

When "trying" to have fun with your kid, several simple rules must be respected. First of all, when you're out horsing around together, you are not allowed to discuss anything difficult or controversial. In other words, any long list of things you want your child to change about him-self or herself must be temporarily abandoned.

Imagine you and your fifteen-year-old son decided to go fishing. You are slowly floating down the river after having caught a couple of cat-fish, enjoying the sun and the calm rocking of the boat in the water. The fish remind you that you're hungry, so you mentally check your pockets for lunch money. There's enough—you're a good provider. Will your son be? Not if he keeps performing like he did on that last science test. You'll set him straight. So you blurt out, "I still can't believe you got a D on that biology exam." The fun is over.

Second, don't even try to take the whole family along if you're going out with your adolescent for some fun. It's much easier to get along with someone when there are fewer people to complicate the situation. Also, parents of adolescents report very frequently that one of their biggest problems is sibling rivalry, and you won't have any fun if you are con-stantly having to keep two kids off each other's back.

In addition, many teenagers have a nasty habit of not wanting to go out with the family because then it isn't cool to be seen by your friends. One thirteen-year-old girl I saw always sat in the back seat, and then hit the floor whenever she thought she saw someone she knew. Don't be offended, this is perfectly natural. Use your don't-take-it-personally strategies. Going out with only one parent may be a little more tolerable for an adolescent.

Third, do something enjoyable together on a regular basis. Often activities have to be planned in advance, which can provide other benefits. If two people know that they are going to do something pleasant together on the weekend, this knowledge will tend to produce a "back-up effect." The idea will help them get along better Monday through Friday.

Finally, try to avoid doing something that the teen likes and you hate. If you are not having a good time at a rock concert, for example, your feeling ill at ease is likely to show. The two of you may then argue or snipe at one another, and the whole experience may be worse than doing nothing at all. Although it isn't always easy, the two of you want to find something that you can both enjoy at the same time.

Is there a sure thing—something an adolescent and his middle-aged parent can usually enjoy together? The closest to a sure thing is going to a movie and then getting something to eat afterward. It's not that difficult to find a movie you can both enjoy, and if you're not getting along too well to begin with, this idea also has the advantage that you don't have to talk to each during the show. Afterward, while you're eating, you can at least discuss the movie a little.

What if your youngster refuses to do anything with you? Try not to act hurt or insulted. Remember that the kid's main job during adolescence is to get ready to leave home for good. Try to be as patient as you can, don't take it personally, and do the best you can with the other tactics for getting along.

Active listening, talking about yourself, shared fun. Aren't these all wonderful ideas? A new relationship in no time! Of course it's not so easy, but neither wishful thinking nor righteous indignation will get you anywhere. If you think you have the energy and time, it's on to the last tactic.

Positive Reinforcement

When you have a bad relationship with anyone, the idea of praising or commending that person for something sounds anywhere from impossible to insane. Yet a sincere compliment is one of the best ways to improve how you get along with an adolescent. Positive reinforcement simply means that you let a teenager know when you think she has done something well. You can say something to her while she's actually doing whatever it is you appreciate, or after she has completed the task. It might sound something like this:

> *"Looks like you put a lot of effort into that paper."*
>
> *"The grass looks real good."*
>
> *"Thanks for helping me move that stuff into the basement."*
>
> *"I can't believe how great your room looks!"*
>
> *"I think you handled that problem with your boyfriend better than I would have in your shoes."*

There's nothing too tricky about making comments like these, but again there are a few points you need to keep in mind. Some kids like effusive, elaborate praise and recognition, while others like a more brief, businesslike approach. By the time they are adolescents, more teens will be in the second category, so it may be best to keep praise short and businesslike. Also, if you're not in the habit of expressing appreciation anyway—or if your relationship is pretty bad, you'd better start out small so your statements don't stand out like sore thumbs. Even if it feels a little awkward and embarrassing, though, just give it a try.

With positive reinforcement, consistency is also important. Consistency can be very difficult, especially when a child irritates you frequently. Some parents have found it's helpful to work a sort of "mini-contract" with themselves, in which they agree they will say three to five positive things per day. Successfully dealing with your attitude about The Snub is important here. If you're feeling rejected all the time, you won't be complimenting anyone.

You've probably heard the old advice about not criticizing the child but criticizing the behavior? Interestingly, the same rule holds when it comes to positive feedback. It is better to point out what the youngster did right and perhaps elaborate on that, rather than to try to say what a wonderful person the adolescent is. The latter approach comes across as inappropriate and embarrassing.

Finally, don't leave your objectivity behind. Some parents say, "There's nothing good to say about the kid!" This assessment is rarely true. There's a book that's been around for a while called *Catch Them Being Good*. The point is that if you are really paying attention and your attitude has been adjusted, you will see lots of things to reinforce.

Where Do You Start?

The strategies in this chapter vary in terms of how much control you have and how much cooperation from the teen is required for success. Where a relationship is somewhat strained, start with tactics over which you have more control.

First, once you're good at not taking things personally, the Four Cardinal Sins must be avoided. Otherwise you might as well not bother with the other tactics. The good news, though, is that the Four Cardinal Sins are under your direct control. You don't need the teenager's help to stop your own nagging or lecturing. The next tactic that you largely control is positive reinforcement. Do it in short bursts—hopefully with enthusiasm—in the beginning. The teen doesn't even have to respond. Next, don't just focus all your attention on your teen. Relax, let your hair down and talk about yourself some. Let the kids know you're human and imperfect and that there's more to you than your job as a parent. All the kids have to do is stick around briefly for your stories.

Then sympathetic listening might be used to good effect, but it requires more input from the kids. For a parent, listening in this way takes practice, but it is extremely helpful in getting along (excellent for marriages, too).

If you get this far successfully, you'll be doing pretty well in improving your relationship and you can take a shot at shared fun. It will be easier because you'll be communicating much better, and there will be much less chance of unpleasant surprises.

> **SOLUTION: Silent Sue**
> In this chapter we've learned some potential strategies for dealing with Silent Sue. Sue's doing the normal teen pulling away, so Mom is going to first try some sympathetic listening and some positive reinforcement. Then Mom is going to cross her fingers and try to get her daughter to go to the movies with her.

PART V

Take Care of Yourself

CHAPTER 15

Midlife Parent

If you are old enough to have teenage sons and daughters, you are old enough to be at a point referred to as midlife: thirty-five, forty, fifty or beyond. For many adults this age involves the painful realization that they now have more experience than dreams—the exact opposite of adolescent psychology. The respective mental states might look something like this:

ADOLESCENT　　　　　**PARENT**

What's more, the realities and experience are certainly not all they were once cracked up to be. The career that once held such great promise may not have produced the desired financial rewards, status or satisfaction. Even for those who are successful, each morning demands getting out of bed for a repeat performance. Other folks feel a longing, after fifteen or twenty years at the same job, for something different.

Of all the cherished dreams of childhood and adolescence, perhaps the one that takes the greatest beating with the passage of time involves love and marriage. In recent years the divorce rate has hovered at slightly less than fifty percent. Large numbers of mothers—and more and more fathers—are single parents. Many of the couples who remain together do so for reasons of finances, children, lifestyle and so on— even if they are not especially happy with their relationship with their spouse. If you add it all up, the odds of experiencing a satisfying marriage may be substantially better than fifty percent *against* you— a far cry from the old "and they lived happily ever after" feeling Rapunzel and many other people had on the day they got married.

Midlife also brings increasing health problems and a greater consciousness that life won't last forever, what one writer called a sense of "the dark at the end of the tunnel." Mom and Dad's own parents may have died already or may suffer from serious health problems, making these realities even more graphic. The awareness, for example, that many of your favorite childhood actors, actresses and singers are dead, or that you are now older—rather than younger—than almost all the major active sports figures, can give you the uneasy feeling that life is more than half over. This realization certainly does not mean that all parents of teens are depressed, but it does mean that—at this point in their lives—parents of adolescents will be experiencing stresses that are regular, sizeable, fairly abundant and predictable.

On top of all this, these midlife parents have to tolerate, get along with, stay in touch with, and sometimes manage a changing adolescent.

How Are You Doing?

How well you handle the normal irritations as well as the bigger problems you encounter with an adolescent will depend a lot on how well you are doing in the first place. Take a moment to evaluate yourself at this point in time. Think of three dimensions: daily stress, usual mood and self-esteem. If you had to rate yourself on a scale from 1 to 5, how would you come out? Imagine a scale that goes like this:

5	4	3	2	1
LIFE IS GREAT	THINGS ARE PRETTY GOOD	I'M DOING OK	THINGS ARE NOT SO HOT	LIFE IS AWFUL

If you gave yourself a rating of 4 to 5, you feel happy most of the time and generally satisfied with your existence (no one is happy all the time). Your job and relationships with your spouse and important other people can provide stress, but the stress you experience is usually challenging and nothing you can't handle. You normally find your activities rewarding and you have fun on a regular basis. Even though you know you're not perfect, you are aware that basically you're a decent and competent person, and you know that other people also appreciate these qualities in you.

A parent falling in the average range (3) feels that life is so-so or OK. Sometimes this parent feels fine about things, at other times not so good. She experiences a fair amount of stress and occasionally is not so sure how to handle it. She can have fun, which includes doing things with other people. Her perception of herself is that she's about average, and she is aware of significant weaknesses in her behavior or personality that bother her.

A rating of 2 to 1 here means that life is bad or even the pits. This midlife parent usually feels down and/or burned out. Problems that he has are generally overwhelming and he doesn't feel at all capable of handling them. He doesn't have a lot of fun and tends to avoid spending much time with other people. His self-esteem is low or nonexistent. Often he sees himself as being nobody or as being useless.

In making these ratings try to think as objectively as possible. Often middle-aged adults, when thinking about age and aging, tend to go to extremes. They either joke around all the time or they get excessively morbid. What is the reality of your life right now?

Dreamer Meets Disillusioned

What happens when Dreamer—the young adolescent—meets Disillusioned—the midlife parent? It's hard to imagine a worse combination! These people are supposed to live together, get along and try to resolve problems!? Many adolescents and their parents do get along very well, of course, but there are still some common problems that parents can run into when their children reach the teen years.

Parents were once adolescents themselves. Almost all adults have fairly vivid memories of what their teenage years were like. When their children reach that same stage of life, Mom and Dad often find that their children's adolescence triggers "old tapes" or memories of some of their own past successes or conflicts. Sometimes parents overidentify with their children's pain and try too hard to help. But an overly anxious parent will invariably aggravate a teenager! The parents' constant worrying about an adolescent will produce arguments, misunderstandings and a tremendous amount of domestic conflict.

In addition, Mom and Dad may remember all the things they did as teenagers that their parents didn't know about. They then begin to worry about what their kids are up to, thus making themselves too suspicious and also, perhaps, too inquisitive—like our Dad who committed the Four Cardinal Sins in the front door scene.

Most parents also see their children as reflections of—and on—themselves. It is certainly no fun to feel that your self-esteem is in the hands of someone else, especially if that someone else seems so committed to being different from you. Do I want to take him to our friend's house for dinner when he dresses the way he does?

Finally, the relationship between Dreamer and Disillusioned can be strained by something else. By the time a child hits adolescence, the job of parenting him is about seventy per cent over. It's definitely getting late. Some parents, for example, look at their seventeen-year-old son and don't like what they see: strange hair, sloppy clothes, pierced body parts and a sullen attitude. In a state of near panic, the parents then attempt "crash courses"—last-ditch attempts to shape up or modify the kid before he escapes the house for good.

These attempts often involve long lectures, scoldings or arguments. Sometimes the kid is unnecessarily dragged off to a shrink. These efforts are rarely successful. It's almost as if the parents see themselves as manufacturers of some kind. The child is their product. He's getting close to the end of the assembly line, but he's not at all what he's supposed to be. Better get in there quick and fix something!

Emotional Dumping

There are, of course, times when parents of adolescents must take charge, intervene and do something assertive in their kids' interests—whether the teens like the idea or not. Our focus here, however, is on unnecessary parental intrusions—intrusions that are based more on *parental stress* than on *problem severity*. Parents who are too stressed out themselves are notorious for getting super upset from The Snub, and then repeatedly using the Four Cardinal Sins on their kid's MBAs.

Believe it or not, the first step in getting along with any adolescent is to make sure that you're OK. If earlier you rated yourself as not doing too well, it is very important that you attend to your own problems first. After you get yourself back on track, you can worry again about your teenager if you really need to.

If you are not doing well, there are several reasons why taking care of yourself first is a good idea. One reason for taking care of yourself first is this: If you are really stressed-out, you will not be

> **QUIK TIP**
>
> Parents who are too stressed-out themselves are notorious for getting super upset from The Snub and then repeatedly using the Four Cardinal Sins on their kid's MBAs.

able to talk about any problems without getting very upset. You will just be too sore. You will do more damage to your relationships with others, and it's not very likely you'll solve anything.

A second reason for taking care of yourself is quite simple: why should you spend another hour of your life feeling unnecessary pain if there's something you can do about it?

Finally, if you are in bad shape, perhaps the biggest problem you will experience is one that is invisible. It is called "displacement." Displacement is kind of a fancy term for what is otherwise known as "emotional dumping." It refers to our uncanny tendency to transfer feelings from one situation to another—without really being aware of what we are doing. A father who has just been chewed out by his boss at work, for example, may return home and yell at his wife because their three-year-old left her tricycle in the driveway.

The odd thing about emotional dumping, however, is that while Dad is yelling at his wife, he will actually feel and believe that the bike is the problem. The real source of his being so stressed-out—what happened at work—will in a way be "unconscious" to him, or more or less forgotten. His wife, of course, will also believe that the tricycle is the problem, unless she gets more information about what happened to him at work.

Displacement, therefore, actually involves two things: 1) an exaggeration of the seriousness of a problem, and 2) a focus on the wrong problem. How does this apply to handling a problem with an adolescent? If you are really doing poorly yourself, you will tend to have an exaggerated view of the seriousness of your teen's problems. Every little thing will seem like a big deal, even though it may not be. You might, for example, start thinking of an average teen as some kind of walking catastrophe. You may also get extremely upset about minor problems (MBAs), such as a messy room or a lot of time spent on the phone.

Perhaps worst of all, you might not realize that the biggest source of your distress is you, the midlifer, and not your child. If your teenager has some sense that displacement is going on—that she is basically OK and you are overreacting to her minor offenses—she will begin to resent you more and more.

War!

Kids can also dump or displace their negative feelings about life in general onto their parents, just as parents can do theirs onto the kids. If the dumping starts going both ways, it can produce a permanent state of war. In a sense, war is worse than The Snub and Resnub, because it can involve active hostility. War makes adolescents even more dangerous to themselves and their communities.

A number of years ago, in a book called *Games People Play*, Eric Berne described some of the goofy ways that people interact with each other, and he labeled these unproductive transactions "games." A game always had some superficial plausibility to it, according to Berne, but underneath, the "player" was really trying to accomplish something else—often some hidden, self-serving and emotional objective.

Berne used somewhat odd, humorous titles for his games, such as "Kick Me" and "Why Does This Always Happen to Me?!" What was probably the most common of these games he called "Now I've Got You, You Son-of-a-Bitch!" In this game one person repeatedly catches another doing something wrong, and then proceeds to have an enjoyable temper tantrum—scolding, blasting or lecturing his target for the supposed horrible transgression.

The plausible part of "Now I've Got You" is that something was done that was not so hot, and that behavior might need to be pointed out or corrected. The hidden part of the game, though, is the emotional satisfaction the chief player gets out of venting his spleen and having a well-justified, much deserved, self-righteous tantrum. And if life isn't going so well for you, a tantrum can be kind of fun!

Here's the deal on anger. Of all the negative emotions—anxiety, guilt, depression and anger—anger is somewhat unique. No one ever enjoys feeling anxious or guilty. A few people can enjoy feeling a little depressed, especially when they feel sorry for themselves. But lots of people can enjoy being angry—not all the time necessarily, but it can be quite satisfying now and then to blow up.

In fact, repeat this angry diagnose-then-blast behavior for a while and it's possible to "get high" on anger and eventually get addicted to it. And what better creature to give a parent their regular anger "fix" than some obnoxious adolescent, especially if the kid also is doing The Snub and also playing his own version of "Now I've Got You."

So if you've totally had it and want to become an accomplished "Now I've Got You" player rather than just your average crabby mother or father, here are some suggestions:

1. Think of your adolescent as a total problem child, even though he's really average or competent.

2. Always find something to criticize the teen for, no matter how small (a sign of success here is that your son always leaves the room when you enter).

3. Constantly evaluate and diagnose the child; keep a sharp look out for any signs of something that is either wrong or just plain irritating.

4. Voice all your worries about him to him. Be consistent.

5. If you have had an especially rotten day, get loaded at night, see the teen as the source of all your problems, then have a royal fit.

6. Constantly work on maintaining the exalted mental state of Righteous Indignation.

There are also other tactics that frustrated parents have found successful for ruining relationships with their adolescent children. If the kid's not around, you can go check his room for drugs, birth control devices, or just plain messiness. During conversations you can use clever arguments and interruptions to make his thinking look stupid, as well as listen in on his phone conversations or try to find a diary to get more ammunition.

Seriously, if you feel you might be getting into a state of war with your teenager, take our simple Anger Addiction Test. Answer these three questions:

1. Am I getting quite angry at this child on a regular basis?

2. Am I going out of my way to find things to get mad about?

3. Do I enjoy blowing up at this kid?

Although it may be hard, try to be as honest as you can. If you answered "Yes" to these questions, you are probably addicted to anger and you are either in—or about to be in—a state of war with your own offspring. That means you are deluding yourself that your "corrective efforts" are geared toward helping the child shape up. Your real underlying motive is to play "Now I've Got You" and your adolescent is now officially dangerous.

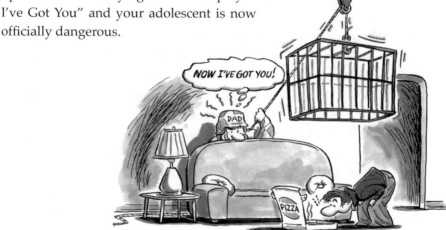

CHAPTER 16

How To Take Care of Yourself

If you are in bad shape and you are contributing constantly to a state of war with a teenager, something should be done. But what? Here are some different aspects of your life that you may want to take a look at.

Your mind. Perhaps it would be a good idea to get yourself into counseling or psychotherapy. Lots of people have done it, and often with very good results. Research has proven over and over that depression, anxiety and a whole host of other problems can be significantly altered through counseling with the right kind of professional. Sometimes certain kinds of medications can also be useful. Though some people still feel that mental health treatment carries a stigma of some kind, that point of view is fading and is being replaced by a more practical attitude.

If you do find a counselor, make sure you like him or her. If you don't feel comfortable after two or three sessions, go find somebody else. Remember that you have a right to shop around.

You say you don't need any help from a shrink and you'd rather go it alone? These days there are quite a few helpful books that have to do with managing stress and other psychological problems. Perhaps you can talk to a friend or professional to find one that might be good for you.

139

There is a time limit here, though. Give yourself two months, and if you don't feel any better by then, find a professional therapist to talk to.

Your marriage/relationship. Does your marriage need some work? Don't they all? No one's relationship with his or her spouse is perfect, but if this is one of the problems that is bothering you a lot, it might be a good idea to give it some thought. Even if you're not living together, it's still a significant relationship with someone else and so it's a good idea to examine that bond from time to time.

It's one thing to say you will go into marital counseling, but it's a different matter to actually do something about it. For one thing, males frequently don't care for the process very much, and they can be quite resistant to the idea. Also, men and women usually have very different thoughts about what they expect out of their marriage. Women are normally much more interested in things like closeness, companionship, open communication and orientation toward family. (More women than men, for example, will read this book.) Women, therefore, are usually the ones who initiate discussions about problems, as well as attempts at marital therapy.

If you are thinking about marital counseling, here are some suggestions. First, try to pick your counselor together or, if one person is more reluctant to go along, let the reluctant one choose the therapist. Second, go in to see the counselor together the first time if you can (the counselor will usually suggest this anyway). And third, before as well as during any counseling, try to listen respectfully to your spouse's or partner's point of view, even if you don't agree. Research also has shown that marital counseling can be quite helpful—if you can get both parties involved.

Your job. Perhaps the major cause of your stress is not your teenager or your marriage, but your job. At this point in their lives, many parents—mothers and fathers—have been working on the same job for many years. Changing occupations or positions is certainly not easy, but ask yourself several questions. Do you spend a lot of time complaining to others about your work? Do you consistently feel overloaded and unappreciated when you're there? What do you think of your boss, and how do you get along with her? How about coworkers? How do you feel on Sunday nights—or each morning when you wake up and realize it's a work day?

Your body. How about the physical side of your life? You're certainly no spring chicken! What kind of shape are you in? You may be tired of hearing this, but it is very helpful to get regular, vigorous physical exercise three to four times per week, especially if you are routinely feeling anxious, angry or otherwise stressed-out. *A regular exercise regime for yourself is one of the best things you can do for your kids.* If you don't take your frustrations out on the racquetball court, you may very well take them out on your son or daughter. Do you have some physical problem that needs attention, or are you avoiding that physical exam because you are afraid of what the doctor will say? Worry festering in the back of your mind will make you even more irritable.

QUIK TIP

A regular exercise regime for yourself is one of the best things you can do for your kids. If you don't take your frustrations out on the racquetball court, you may very well take them out on your son or daughter.

Pass the Buck?

Taking care of yourself may even mean that you temporarily pass the buck to your spouse when it comes to dealing with your troublesome teenager. This temporary renunciation of responsibility will make you feel guilty, but keep in mind that—if you are in terrible emotional shape—you would probably make things worse by trying to intervene in an adolescent's life.

You may feel that your spouse may not be as conscientious as you would be in trying to handle a problem. It's too bad you feel that way, but unless there is an emergency, if you're all stressed out it's time to avoid getting involved. Some people say that's why God made two parents, so if one is out of commission, the other can take over.

What if you don't have a spouse anymore and you simply have an "ex"? See if your ex can help out with the child, and if he or she can't, try to find a counselor for both you and your teen. If you do try to work out something with your ex, it may require laying to rest a lot of old hostilities, so make sure you're prepared to make an honest effort.

If you do finally get your act together and start feeling better, what is the first thing you should do with your adolescent? Nothing! Go back and reevaluate the situation to see if you still think there is major cause for concern. MBAs are aggravating even if you're in good shape, but they're still MBAs!

In our culture there's a kind of kids-first ethic that sometimes makes parents feel guilty if they think of doing things that are in their own, blatant self interest. But think about it for a second: If you rated yourself a 2 or a 1 on our rating scale before, how much fun do you think you are to live with? Maybe not much. The fact of the matter is you may be a walking negative. So call a friend for dinner, get out those walking or jogging shoes, or get yourself a new book—today!

PART VI

Relax and
Enjoy the Movie

CHAPTER 17

Boomerang Kids

Some folks think it's a new phenomenon, but it's not. When the economy is in bad shape and jobs are scarce, more young adults in the 20-to-25-year-old age range move back in with their parents. Some of these young people are high school grads, some have associate degrees, and some have graduated from college. But they all have two things in common: They don't have money and they don't have jobs. These "kids" are often referred to as the "boomerang" generation.

"Well, I'll just live at home for a few years and save some money" at first may sound like a handy, simple and even pleasant proposition. But it's not. It's hard on parents and it's also hard, surprisingly, on the young person moving back in. Except for unusual circumstances, getting back together like this is taxing for everybody.

For one thing, the older folks have grown accustomed to more freedom. They have more living space and the ability to do as they please when they please. If there are other kids still at home, readjustments will be needed in regard to things like living space, schedules, and—most important—food! Mom and Dad have also gotten used to not worrying about someone coming and going all the time. Can I lock the door tonight when I go to bed? Who's using the car tomorrow morning? It may sound terrible to say, but the truth is that the somewhat involuntary return of a child who has been away for a while can be downright irritating and depressing.

But don't kid yourself: The homecoming is not easy for the young adult either. It's not like he can lie around all day, watch TV and then expect to get fed in the evening. Coming back home feels like a failure to many people. How come my friends have jobs, are married and have their own places—and I don't? Coming home, especially after being independent at college or elsewhere, has a distinct feeling of going backwards to it. Back in the familiar surroundings of your old room, you can easily feel like you are ten years old again.

Prevention and Management

Here are several suggestions for avoiding the pain and aggravation associated with this issue. First of all, don't kid yourself that this kind of plan is a good idea and don't suggest it. Only consider it as a last resort.

> **KEY CONCEPT**
>
> Homecoming is not easy for a young adult either. It's not like he can lie around all day, watch TV and then expect to get fed in the evening. Coming back home feels like a failure to many people.

Brainstorm with your son or daughter other options like living with friends, subsidizing their rent temporarily if you can, continuing in school or the military. Prevention is the first option.

Next, if it looks like your child's coming back home is in fact the best or only choice, negotiate the deal before they walk in the door. Remember the written contracts we discussed in Chapter 9? Well, you're going to need a new one! While your daughter is still away at school, for example, email contract drafts back and forth until you get the one you can all agree on. Below are some of the items that should be covered.

Rent. A twenty-something living in your house should pay rent. What do you charge? Take a look at two things: 1) How are your expenses going to change? 2) What would be a typical rent for similar accommodations in your area (you will probably charge less)? What if your young adults don't have any money? They can go look for a temporary job—minimum wage if need be.

Length of "lease." Keep your agreements to six months or less. Why? Because you want it understood that the goal of the arrangement is for the child to move out of the house and to become independent in the near term. It is essential that everyone look at the deal in this manner.

Otherwise, the days turn to months and the months turn to years and you, in effect, have a fourteen-year old living in your house.

House Rules. Back to adolescence! What is the plan going to be for hours, chores, use of the car, clothing, laundry, use of the TV, music, noise, friends over and so on? These issues are not trivial—they are real barn-burners. And the most incendiary of all these apparent trivia is food! Who pays for it, makes it, shares it (or not) and eats it? Deciding how to manage these potential problems may tax your best diplomatic skills!

In setting up your House Rules again, try to respect both your kid's desire for independence as well as your own desire for independence. If your son is twenty-four, for example, maybe he can come in at 1 a.m. provided he doesn't make a lot of racket or wake you up. Maybe it's no problem if he wants to stay out all night with a friend.

But also sympathize with your own desire for freedom. Don't feel you have to babysit. You don't, for example, have to feed your child or always invite her along everywhere you go. You don't have to always ask sympathetic questions or find out how they're progressing along the Great Road of Life. You'll probably find that you'll get less of The Snub than you did when they were teens at home. Even so, it will most likely be a good idea to stay away from the killer of all killers, "How was your day?"

Most kids, of course, will eventually exit the house, succeed in being economically and emotionally independent, and leave your retirement funds intact. In the meantime, carefully negotiate and maintain the terms of your living arrangements and have some fun together. No one ever said this would be easy, so relax and enjoy the movie!

CHAPTER 18

The Future

When the kids finally do leave home, whether at eighteen or twenty-four, it will be a nervous and an exciting time for all. It's like the Big Future is right there staring you all in the face. And even if your kid's off to a good start, all the big jobs we mentioned before still either need to be done or need to be maintained—and that's a life-long task. Staying aloft for your offspring still means finding friends, becoming economically independent, finding and keeping a soulmate, knowing how to enjoy life and so on. Your feelings will ride along with your children's successes and failures.

But the Problem Is Now

But your concern, and ours, in this book is now: living with this teen-ager today. The problem is a family problem but it's also a larger community issue. Today thousands of teens all across the country will snub their parents at the dinner table. Today over one thousand teenage girls will become pregnant without wanting to. And today about twenty people will die in automobile crashes that involve fifteen-to-nineteen-year-old drivers. What can you do about these statistics?

In *Surviving Your Adolescents* we've tried to offer a straightforward blueprint. That strategy can be used to a) help moms and dads deal with their feelings about the rejection and risk problems, b) significantly reduce family turmoil, and c) protect teens and their communities from harm. The same tactics serve all three goals. Remember: The more distant and hostile a parent/teen relationship is, the greater are the risks from driving, drugs, sex and technology. Respectful parent/teen relationships, on the other hand, mean that a community is safer—fewer innocent people get hurt. And finally, open and friendly is a much better and more enjoyable way for a family to live.

So it's time to get to work. In applying the *Surviving Your Adolescents* approach, parents need to take the bull by the horns and not wait for their teens to change. Parents first must alter the way they think about their kids by both understanding adolescence and also by remembering their own teenage years. The most crucial insight in this regard is to appreciate and accept teens' *ferocious desire to run their own lives*.

So stop thinking, "How can they do this to me!?" and start thinking, "Well, I guess The Snub is a normal, healthy adolescent response." Get rid of those upsetting garbage thoughts and turn to more reassuring and realistic common sense:

Depending on how you count them, there are somewhere around 25 million teens in the United States. That adds up to a lot of Snubs, a lot of risk and a lot of potential turmoil. But we need to let teens be teens, and not to try to force them to behave like the young children they used to be, or like adults. And, when you think about it, it might be nice to remain friends with your grown children for the next thirty or forty years. Why not start now?

There's one more reason you might want to take the initiative in getting along better with your adolescents. In ten years or so these teens very likely will produce *your* grandchildren. Grandmothers generally fall in love with the grandkids *before* they're born; grandfathers come along for the ride later. But I can guarantee you this: *Once you've seen a grandkid, you will want to see him or her again.* And if your relationship with your son or daughter stinks, you may be in for some real heartbreak. We've seen it happen lots and lots of times.

So think of all the payoffs—they are very real—and put your nose to the grindstone. Don't take that Snub personally, stick to your House Rules, stay in touch with your teens and take care of yourself as best you can. If all of us parents did that, our lives would feel much better and the dangers from the 25 million teens in this country would be reduced tremendously. We'd have a shot at enjoying the movie. After all, in the grand scheme of things, it's really a very short film.

APPENDIX

Managing Other Issues

Below are some suggestions for handling some common problems that can arise with teens. These ideas are only suggestions, not rules. If you're having trouble with a particular issue, you might consider using these ideas as the basis for a negotiation with your youngster.

Bedtime

Teen sleep deprivation is a big health issue. For the younger thirteen-to-fifteen-year-old crowd, if there is a bedtime problem, the best method is simple advice. If the problem persists, negotiating a bedtime may be the next logical step. If the child persists in going to bed ridiculously late or bothering other family members after the others are in bed, the Major/Minor System may be used. Some really strange sleeping schedules can be related to drug use, depression or tech addictions, so these possibilities may need to be evaluated if the problem continues in spite of every attempt to modify it. For older teens, stay out of their sleeping habits unless the child is disturbing others at night or the teen's sleeping schedule is just so unorthodox that he is obviously suffering from it.

Bumming Around Town

Bumming around town is controversial, but we suggest giving the kids some leeway. During the day or early evening, letting your typical thirteen-to-fifteen-year-olds hang around malls or downtown areas is fine. Ask them to tell you where they are going and make sure hours are clear. Some parents require a call if the kids change places, which is easier these days with cell phones.

Older adolescents can tell you where they think they are going and that's it. No calls are necessary unless they are going out of state or someplace similarly monumental. Parties would be covered by the rules agreed upon for that (see Parties: home and away), and hours must be respected. Don't grill the kid: "Where are you going, with whom, what are you going to do, whose idea was that, what if this happens, how much money do you have, where's your coat it's cold out there and I think you're catching a cold," etc. Your adolescent, you recall, will be less safe if she leaves the house angry with you and so will your neighborhood.

What about kids who have already been having problems while they're out? They are restricted for a while, according to the rules of the Major/Minor System. Then you give the kids some rope, and if they goof up, it's another consequence for a short, defined period. Then let them try again. Under these circumstances, it's hard not to grill the teens before they go out. You are anxious and you want some reassurance but you will just irritate your children with all your questions. And it's much worse when you have an Irritated Problem Kid leaving the house.

Car

There are many possible car arrangements. For more competent teenagers, free use of the automobile (if there are enough cars) is reasonable, and the teen pays for the gas. Competent kids might even be allowed to buy their own car, provided they pay the insurance and their grades stay decent. Many insurance companies have 25 percent discounts for kids who maintain a B average in school. Some families have the adolescent pay the extra premium if she doesn't keep the B average. Don't make this arrangement, though, unless you're sure that your son or daughter is capable of that level of schoolwork in the first place. Linking car use to grades is often a good idea, as long as the deal is defined precisely. For example, the teen can use the car whenever he wishes, provided he maintains a C+ average (2.75 on a four-point system) with no Fs for any quarter or progress report. If he drops below that, the use of the car is restricted temporarily (define the restriction and the time period) until he gets his GPA back to 2.75. If you have a difficult child with marginal school performance, no car on weeknights (except for rare occasions) is a good idea. No drinking and driving, and hours must be respected.

Chores

Negotiation and a family meeting are probably the best place to start with chores. Attempts at advice too often turn into nagging. Sit everyone in the family down, divide the chores up, and if you want, hook up some of the allowance to the chore. Avoid making spontaneous requests about chore-like tasks. Parents are always saying things like, "I only asked you to do one little thing, what's the big deal?" The big deal is that everyone—including parents—hates spontaneous requests.

"But he never does anything he's supposed to!" many parents complain. Some kids are naturally forgetful, while many others naturally resist adult authority. A good option is the Docking System. You have a problem with Mike feeding the dog regularly in the evening, although he had agreed to do it (Mike is fourteen and gets an allowance of $8). Tell him the dog should be fed by 6 p.m. If the dog gets fed, great. If the dog isn't fed by 6 p.m., you will do it, but, you charge 50 cents to do a feeding. If you don't get to it right at 6:05 and Mike beats you to it, there's still no charge. No reminders are allowed! You can use the same procedure for laundry, dishes, kids' stuff lying around the house, and taking out the garbage. Any chore except homework!

Appearance

This is true MBA territory. Keep in mind that for many adolescents their appearance is purposely designed to look weird and to shock you and other adults. Remember how looooong adolescence is and let them have some fun! The best advice is probably to tell the kids that they can wear anything the school will let them in the door with.

Family Outings

A lot of times your teens no longer want to join you on family outings. This change is perfectly normal. For the younger teenagers, working out some kind of a deal may be a good idea, because you may not want to leave them home alone. Punishment for not going may at times be appropriate, but you'll usually have a sullen kid on your hands if you force him to go. Consider doing nothing, leave him home and enjoy yourself!

Older teens can decide for themselves if they want to go with you. There shouldn't be much problem leaving them home by themselves. If they goof up when you're gone (like having a huge, wild party at your house), of course you'd use the Major/Minor program.

Friends and Dating

We suggest staying out of your kids' choice of friends, except under dangerous circumstances. If you don't like some of your children's friends, you might try a little advice or even some negotiating. Part of the problem here is that it is next to impossible to control—especially with older teens who drive—whom your child sees out of the house. In addition, when poor parent/child chemistry exists, your trying to stop a relationship with one of your teen's undesirable friends may only serve to make their bond stronger.

If you can stand it, invite the other kid over to your house and see if you can get to know him. Some of these kids aren't so bad once you spend some time with them! Many parents don't let their kids date until they're 16 years old. Others let the child date, but not alone in a car until they're 16. Parents can chauffeur, or the kids can go out in groups. Violations are handled with the Major/Minor. If your teen is going out on a date, always meet the other party beforehand.

Grades and Homework

With competent children and temporary drops in grades, merely watching and doing some listening might be all that is necessary. Negotiating a positive reward system (like money for grades) has been used with success to help wake the kids up, but the Major/Minor System by itself is not always so useful since it involves only punishment. "You're grounded until you get those grades up!" is a strategy that, if it's going to be used, needs to be very specific (e.g., the grounding ends when you achieve a GPA of 2.5 with no F's). Any motivational system like this, however, should also have some positive reinforcement attached to it. Though rewarding a difficult teenager is never easy for frustrated and angry parents, it works a lot better.

Negotiating set study hours—with no phone interruptions allowed—is often helpful for kids who are struggling. Believe it or not, many adolescents can study better with their radios on (it blocks out other distracting noises), but never with the TV. Do not check the child's work all the time. If you insist on this perverse procedure, be sure to use a lot of positive reinforcement and don't insist on perfection. If all this fails, a professional evaluation, and perhaps psychological testing, may be necessary. Coming up with a diagnosis of learning disability, Attention Deficit Disorder or something else may shed light on the situation, but remember that by the time they're teenagers, a lot of water has already passed under the bridge.

Hours

Hours should be clear for all ages, though for kids in the 16-to-18 group who are generally doing well, considerable flexibility is OK, as long as it's not abused. For younger teens, staying in on weeknights during the school year is a good idea for average or difficult kids, unless there is some special reason for them to go out. With competent kids, going out is not a problem, and you might use the bumming around suggestions above.

What hours are reasonable? We usually suggest sticking with local curfews. This often means something like 11 p.m. on Sunday through Thursday and midnight on Friday or Saturday, and this kind of setup also takes a little of the burden off parents.

What about violations? For first-time offenses, just give the kid some friendly advice. With continued problems, however, a handy and simple system is the following:

1. 15 minute grace period.

2. If he is over 15 minutes late, the child must "pay back" the minutes next time he goes out—he must come in that much earlier. If he was 25 minutes late, for example, he must come in 25 minutes early the next time.

3. Over 45 minutes late, he must pay back double time.

4. Over three hours late, one week grounding or consider it a Medium or Major offense.

Don't grill the adolescent when he comes in late: "Where were you?" "Why can't you ever get home on time?" etc. You may just be asking for a lot of lies or other forms of verbal refuse, which makes it harder for everyone to get to sleep afterwards. Inform him of the consequences the next morning.

Meals and Eating Habits

Rigid adherence to attendance at nightly family dinners is less and less appropriate as the child gets older. Suggesting that he be present at four of seven evening meals each week might be a reasonable idea, but his not showing up should not trigger the Major / Minor System. It might be better to go back to merely being an observer. Nagging about coming to the dinner table is not allowed, no matter what you cooked.

What the child eats should be handled the same way. Suggesting that he eat three of the four foods available often works well, but if the teen wants something else, the answer is either "No" or "OK, but you'll have to get it, pay for it and make it yourself." Will the adolescent clean up the kitchen after he cooks something for himself? Of course not. Use the Docking System if you get stuck with his mess.

Sloppy eating habits have never been nagged away. Try some friendly advice. If that fails and the kid's really obnoxious, don't eat together. Attendance at meals and manners are not earthshaking issues; and with problem children, trying to do something about these concerns is often more trouble than it's worth.

Messy Rooms

Close the door and don't look. This is perhaps the all-time classic MBA. Her room is her territory and there is no research demonstrating a relationship between sloppy rooms in childhood and lack of success, homelessness or criminal activity in adulthood. Two problems arise here: dirty dishes and laundry. If she doesn't get her laundry down to the washing machine once a week on Saturday morning, it doesn't get washed, or she can do it herself. Teens should learn to do their own laundry anyway, since their parents already have enough to do. If you have to pick up dirty dishes from her bedroom, just charge her ten or fifteen cents per item and forget about it.

Money, Allowance, Loans

Allowances are helpful for two reasons. First, they can be used as incentives for chores and other tasks. Second, they can be handy when fines or the Docking System are being used (such as for swearing), and you would like total control over the consequences.

Consider continuing the allowance even if the teen gets a job (you may need some clout), and by all means, encourage her to get a job as soon as she is old enough. It's great for her independence and for her self-esteem. One caution: some research indicates that teens who are in school should not work more than 20 hours per week during the school year.

It's preferable not to get involved in how your adolescent spends his money. Let him learn through trial and error the benefits of saving vs.

the pitfalls of impulsive spending. In situations where the kids are planning to go to college, many parents require that the child save one half of all earnings for his college expenses.

If you are not telling the child how to spend his money, you also should not regularly provide "loans" to bail him out when he's short. There's no problem with helping your teen out on occasion. But when these so-called loans become gifts, you will be subsidizing irresponsibility. If you do make loans, keep them small and set up a strict payback schedule. Make sure it's clear to begin with whether the money is a loan or a gift, and don't make additional loans until the first one is paid back. If the kid is defaulting, garnish his allowance.

Music

Trying to control the quality or nature of the music the children listen to is probably a lost cause. Trying to deal with its volume may not be. Of course, if you are strange enough yourself that you too enjoy your adolescent's musical preferences, then there is no problem. Advice can get tedious and quickly turn into nagging: "Turn that blankity-blank thing down!" If you don't like this noise pollution, negotiate a deal such as sharing the cost of a headset. When someone else is home, for example, the youngster must wear the headset. If that doesn't work, small fines may be more useful. If fines fail, temporary removal of the stereo (e.g., one-day removal after three unsuccessful warnings in one day) should follow.

Negative Attitude

Some kids, it seems, were born crabby. They just appear always to be in a bad mood or to have a chip on their shoulders most of the time. Many other people—adults included—are generally in good spirits, except in the morning. One of the worst things you can do is try to cheer up one of these non-morning people. Your "Isn't this going to be a nice day!" at 6:50 a.m. will be met with the unprintable. Let your child stagger around unmolested.

If the negative attitude is something new and persistent, consider some gentle active listening to see what's going on, or even professional counseling if the attitude appears serious, quite different and enduring. Remember that continued irritability is frequently a sign of depression in kids. Never chase a martyr, however. If the teen is nonverbally "broadcasting" that he is upset about something, and your "What's wrong?" questions are always met with "Nothing," you are stuck. Instead, say "It looks like something's on your mind. If you want to talk about it, let me know." Then turn around and walk away.

Parties: Home and Away

For younger adolescents, parties are no problem if you're there. For older, competent kids with whom you get along well, you might allow a party if you're not home only for extremely limited numbers. Use negotiating first to clarify ground rules, and don't go too far away! Explain what to do if the party gets out of hand (for instance, call the police), then ask your kids if they would really take these actions if they became necessary.

No drinking is allowed. If you find out later that someone was drinking, that person either spends the night or gets a ride home. If your own party is crashed by too many people and you can't handle it, call the police. If you've had repeated problems with parties in the past, just say "No" when your teens request another one, explain once and prepare for testing.

Kids any age can be allowed to go to a party where the parents are home. Call beforehand to make sure the parents will be there. Expect a good deal of flak from your child about this, and comments like, "All my friends think you guys are weird. Everybody else is going." If the parents aren't going to be home, your kids don't go to the party. Imagine you have a troublesome child who wants to go to a party where the parents won't be home. You tell him no. He accuses you of not trusting him. You tell him nicely that he is correct.

Swearing

If you're modeling the words you're telling your kids not to use, you've got a problem. You can't very well tell teenagers not to use certain words when you do in front of them. Some families set up a "swear jar" and simply fine anyone, parents included, for bad language. Anyone who swears has to put 25 or 50 cents in the jar; at the end of the week the money is donated to church or charity. This method seems to work well for many families; in fact, the kids enjoy turning the tables on their parents occasionally and this setup also motivates them not to swear themselves.

Using Your Things

Kids borrow clothes, misplace tools and use up your makeup, deodorant and shampoo. They also like your glasses, wristbands, jogging shoes, diet pop and pens. This type of "borrowing" usually is not a big deal, so in many cases some friendly consultation may be adequate. Why not consider it a compliment—the little creatures are identifying with you!

Nagging and screaming do no good at all. How "Awful" is it, really? Rate it from 0 to 100 on the Awful Scale before you do anything. If you have a chronic problem, try to negotiate some kind of deal or simply outlaw the use of your stuff. Violations may be handled with simple fines. If all else fails, borrow some of their stuff.

Work

Getting and holding down a job is an excellent experience for teenagers. It's a great introduction to the real world and can do wonders for a person's self-esteem. Teens with jobs have their own money and learn something about responsibility, supervision and getting along with others. A job can also help them get out of bed in the morning during the summer. If the teen is looking for a job, don't nag her about it. You may circle job ads in the newspaper if she doesn't find this assistance irritating.

If your son or daughter has problems at work, you should stay out of the situation if you can, though active listening and lots of positive reinforcement may be helpful. Occasionally a supervisor may call you about a problem your adolescent is having. It's a good idea to try to stay out of the middle. If you can, tell your adolescent who called and what the person called about, and then ask your teenager how she thinks she will handle things.

INDEX